Radical

Resiliency

DAVID

OVR COM !

STy WM

Radical

Resiliency

STEPS FOR CLIMBING TO NEW HEIGHTS REGARDLESS OF LIFE'S CHALLENGES

A memoir of personal transformation

by
Steve Welker
and
Kristina Welker, PsyD., LPC

Radical Resiliency

PRINT ISBN-13: 978–0-9968915-2-3
E-BOOK ISBN: 978-0-9968915-3-0
Copyright 2015, 2016
Stephen I. Welker and Kristina D. Welker
All rights reserved

Inquiries should be made to:
Radical Resiliency Publishing
Chandler, AZ
Contact: stevewelker@cox.net
Online at: www.radicalresiliency.com

Cover illustration and production:
Dino Design
Phoenix, AZ
Contact: dino@dinodesign-o.com
Online at: www.dinodesign-o.com

Printed digitally in the United States of America

Contents

About the Cover

To overcome setbacks in life, you need a steadfast commitment, a positive attitude, and a strong support team. The simple cover illustration consists of three elements that represent this journey. The ladder that leads upward to the tree depicts the path that you need to ascend from trials to triumph. The two-sided tree signifies two ways you can emerge after facing a challenge: giving up, therefore withering and dying, or growing, blooming and thriving in spite of the challenge. The clear, blue sky represents hope.

The cover was designed by Dino Paul, a graphic designer, and owner of Dino Design, who is a lifelong friend of mine. For those of you who read my book, *The World at My Fingertips*, you will remember Dino as the snow-skiing instructor who cut me no slack because of my blindness—just as it should be.

An Author's Note

I really struggled with the direction in which I should take this book. My book, *The World at My Fingertips: My personal story of triumph over tragedy*, was just that—the memoir of my life before and after the auto accident that left me blind. So much has happened since I released the book in 2006, I believe that I need to add to the personal story.

On the other hand, I feel that I have learned so much about resiliency that I want to share with readers how you can embrace the tools to overcome any trials that you are facing. I share these skills with people who attend my 'Radical Resiliency' seminars. To come clean right up front, these are not skills I dreamed up on my own. I am an insurance agent, after all. What do I really know about resiliency? Yes, I overcame a major tragedy, but could I effectively explain the concept?

So, my resident expert entered the picture, Dr. Kristina Welker. (She will always be Kristi to me).

For those of you who read my book, you will recall that I spoke of a wonderful woman who is also my amazing wife. Dr. Kristina has a doctorate in psychology, a masters in counseling, a Bachelors in Communications and is a licensed professional counselor in Arizona. She wrote her doctoral thesis on resiliency.

So we collaborated on this book. The first three chapters are the Welker story, the family update, and a chapter introducing my amazing new guide dog, Orbit. Using Dr. Kristina's thesis as a blueprint, and her counseling experiences of helping clients effectively navigate through life's challenges, we were able to develop our message of Radical Resiliency. We believe that with the two of us partnering, we can help readers put a 'face' to the concept. So this is no dry self-help book. Instead, it is a how-to book by two people who have faced enormous challenges and have been able to overcome them.

Just a quick note about the writing style we've chosen. It is delivered in a first-person style; that is, from my point of view. But, don't be mistaken. It is truly a combined effort by both Dr. Kristina and me.

Rather than change the narrative to third-person when we transition from our family story to the key concepts of Radical Resiliency, we decided to continue the first-person writing style. We did this to make the text flow consistently and thus make it easier for readers to follow. We realize from our own experiences as readers, that it is awkward when a book switches from one person's viewpoint to that of another—or worse, when it is written in the dreaded third person. I hope you will agree with our decision.

Dedication

This book is dedicated to our incredible boys,
Dylan and Colton.

After our near-fatal accident, our sons gave us so many reasons to live. They gave us reasons to smile as they performed in their Christmas plays, played baseball in their little league games and rode Pirates of the Caribbean dozens of times. They gave us reasons to laugh at their childhood antics and great senses of humor. They gave us reasons to worry as they began to spread their wings and gain independence. They gave us reasons to be frustrated as they made mistakes. They gave us reasons to cry when they fought their own battles. And reasons to be proud when they overcame those challenges. We are gratified by the incredibly difficult job that we fulfilled as parents. In good times and in bad, our sons have given us many reasons to be resilient!

Acknowledgments

There is an old saying that goes, "If the Good Lord's willing and the creek don't rise." That motivational quip kept us going as we wrote this book. So, first and foremost, we would like to acknowledge the "Good Lord" for providing us with the ability, the dedication and the patience to complete this book. With God, all things are possible.

Along that line, we would like to thank the many Christian mentors, who have helped us in our walk: those who have been formally trained in the vocation and those who simply possess the gift of teaching.

We also appreciate the many friends and family members who have supported us, both emotionally and physically, through the many years since our life-altering accident that changed our lives forever. Without their love and compassion this book would not have been possible.

And finally, a special thanks to Lamar and Janice Welker, Steve's parents, who have provided us with unconditional love and support as we pushed through our pain and transcended to new heights.

Prologue

The Back Story

For those of you who did not read my book, *The World at My Fingertips: My personal story of triumph over tragedy*, where have you been living? Under a rock? But seriously, I do think it was pretty good use of several hundred trees or kilowatts of electricity, depending upon whether you read the print edition or the e-book.

At any rate, if you did miss the book, or if it has been a while since you read it, I think it is important to briefly recap our personal story. I read it recently to refresh my memory and was reminded of what we have been through and how far we have come.

Before that horrific day in April of 1994, I had led a pretty charmed life. I was born and raised in Phoenix, Arizona by Lamar and Janice Welker, who were bankers. I was that prototypical suburban latchkey kid of the 1960s. So it goes without saying that there was never a dull moment around our house for us kids, Jim and Cheryl (older brother and sister) and Janice (spoiled little sister).

After attending public schools and learning the ABCs, something about Dick and Jane, and how to do as little as possible and still graduate, I attended Scottsdale Community College. It was my introduction to higher learning, and those years were some of the best years of my life. From there, it was off to Arizona State University for a degree in business.

Diploma in hand, I began my illustrious career in the property and casualty insurance field. First, I spent a couple of years running my dad's (Lamar Welker) Sedona office. Then, I was responsible for the accounting while I lived in Phoenix.

Next, I went to Westfield, an insurance carrier with home offices in Ohio. A year of freezing my nose off ended when this Arizona boy was mercifully transferred to Orange County, California.

After thawing out on the beaches for a few years, I was transferred to Tucson (no easy assignment for this Sun Devil!), and eventually back to Phoenix. And what did I learn from all my travels? You can come to love it anywhere, depending on your attitude. This knowledge would serve me well in the future—more than I could ever have imagined.

In Phoenix, I was living the life; 'tall cotton', as they say. I was the personification of a YUPPIE—a young urban professional. I was making good money, had many friends, drove a cool car, owned a home, and hung out at the trendy clubs. I was all that and more, or so I thought. Before I knew it, I was thirty-four, still single and with no prospects in sight. My friends were getting married, starting families, and generally growing up. I appeared to be on the road to eternal bachelorhood.

As fate would have it, on a Friday night in May of 1991, my life changed forever. I was introduced to the woman of my dreams. My search was over. I devoted an entire chapter of meeting Kristi in my book. If you are a hopeless romantic, please read it. It's some of my best work. The long and short of Kristi is this: stunning blue eyes, infectious smile, and beautiful—inside and out. We were married the following year and I never looked back.

Nearly two years after we were married, on April 30, 1994, driving down the road on a bright and sunny morning in the desert, we were filled with excitement and trepidation. A long and miraculous journey was entering its final stage. We were on our way to the airport to meet our surrogate, who was carrying our biological twin babies. Then our plan was to fly to a California hospital for the birth of our miracle boys. We were floating on air, and we were trying hard to act as if everything was normal, and it was—until a split second later.

I noticed ahead of us, traveling in the opposite direction, on the other side of a median strip, a policeman in a slow speed

2

pursuit. I quickly slowed down and pulled my brand new Jeep Cherokee onto the sidewalk, assuming the approaching car chase would pass us. Unfortunately, that is not what happened.

What we did not know at the time was that the officer was following a car which was driven by an impaired driver (diabetic coma). Suddenly, without any warning, the vehicle accelerated to about 50 miles an hour, jumped the center median, and hit us head on. There was absolutely nothing I could do but grip the steering wheel and brace for the impact.

The violent collision literally tossed our jeep into the air, rolled it several times and caused it to land on its roof in the middle of the intersection. The driver compartment was crushed. It is a miracle Kristi and I were not killed on impact.

Kristi had to be extricated from the vehicle by EMTs. She was taken to a nearby hospital with an extensive list of injuries. She had broken both of her clavicles, crushed her left foot, and suffered closed-head injuries from which she suffered for several years.

I was taken by helicopter to another hospital, where the receiving medical staff, after inspecting my broken body, believed that I would not survive through the night. My family was contacted and advised to come to the hospital to say their final good-byes. As a result of the incredible force with which my head had hit the steering wheel, I had broken virtually every bone in my face. I was bleeding profusely and had lost a great deal of blood. The most critical injury, however, was that my brain had swelled because I suffered a traumatic brain injury (TBI). To relieve the swelling, a shunt was inserted into my brain. This helped the immediate problem, but I was not out of the woods—not by a long shot.

The next several days were touch and go. I was put into a drug-induced coma to stabilize my body and to improve my chances of healing. The doctors—and my family—would have to wait until I came out of the coma to evaluate the extent of my injuries. The doctors voiced serious concerns that I would likely need to learn how to walk and talk again...if I survived.

After twelve days in the coma, my vital signs improved enough for the doctors to bring me back to consciousness. They were relieved (and extremely surprised!) to find that my cognitive and motor skills appeared to be much better than they had anticipated. However, due to the severe swelling of my brain and the pressure on my optic nerve, the nerve had suffered an incurable stroke. I was permanently blind.

Here is how it was explained to my parents and me. The optic nerve connects the eye to the visual cortex of the brain. It is, in a sense, the super-highway that takes all of the images the eye detects and sends them to the brain for processing. Because my optic nerve was dead, that vital roadway was now closed for all traffic. I was, barring a miracle, never going to see another thing for the rest of my life.

This wasn't supposed to happen to me. Steve Welker was not supposed to be blind. The man who had led such a charmed life was not supposed to live the rest of his days in darkness. Not now. Not so soon after he had met and married the woman of his dreams. Not just before the birth of his miracle babies.

About the same time, I was coming out of my coma, our miracle baby boys, Colton and Dylan, were born. It wasn't the homecoming we had planned. Kristi was in a wheelchair, her left foot in a cast after microsurgery had saved her foot and unfortunately, because her clavicles were broken, she was unable to pick up our newborn babies. Suffering from her own brain injury, she wasn't thinking very clearly, but she became hyper-focused about my care and found the doctors who were considered by many, to be the best reconstructive surgeons in the valley.

I have no memory of being told that I was a father. With my severe brain injury, I barely knew who I was. What should have been one of the most memorable days of my life was lost in the damaged memory cells of my fragile brain.

The first order of business in terms of my own recovery was a nine-hour surgery to rebuild my face. This was a rather remarkable procedure intended to make me look somewhat like myself again. I was left with nineteen titanium plates embedded at various locations in my face. Every single plate required screws to hold them in place. Beyond that, surgery was necessary to remove a portion of my skull to rebuild my nose. That procedure produced a nifty scar across my head, from ear to ear, with its seam held together by staples. I must have looked like Frankenstein's monster.

For the next two months, I remained confined in the hospital, attempting to heal, and I began to adjust to my new life as a blind person. My days were filled with occupational therapy, vocational therapy, physical therapy, and a seemingly never-ending stream of nurses, doctors, family, and dozens of well-wishers. All of this activity, coupled with the energy it took for my body to heal, left me feeling totally exhausted all of the time.

At some point during my healing process I recognized that the mantra, "You are never too old to need your mother", was definitely true. Due to Kristi's injuries and the new babies, it was extremely difficult for her to visit me. So, that was when my mom stepped in.

My mom, Janice Welker, moved into a hotel near the hospital so she could tend to her broken son. Mom was at the hospital every day, making sure I ate my meals. She steadfastly, religiously monitored doctors and therapists visits and carefully controlled the number of visitors I had. I honestly believe that if not for my mom I never would have left that hospital.

But leave I did. The question was: to where? I returned to the same house I had left on that beautiful April morning some two months before. But all of the anticipation and excitement I would have normally experienced by having twin boys in the house, was not there. I was now a broken, damaged man. My successful career was gone. My hopes and dreams of fatherhood had been destroyed. And what about my marriage? Could I really expect Kristi to stay with me? I would not have blamed her one bit if she chose to pack up the boys and move on. Mentally, that's where I was. I felt I had nothing to live for.

One night, shortly after my return home, while sitting on the couch with Kristi, I reached one of those penultimate moments in my life, one that changed everything forever. The boys were sitting in their high chairs, laughing and cooing with each other. It suddenly hit me like a ton of bricks! These boys needed a dad. Though I was broken and damaged, my boys still needed a dad, and I suddenly, truly believed that their father should be me. And their mom, Kristi, needed a husband. Maybe I wasn't going to be the man she had originally bargained for, but I was still the man she married. I still loved her and she still loved me.

I decided that night that I would make this work. I had to pick up the pieces of my shattered life, put them back together as best I could, and be the father and husband God intended me to be. I decided that I didn't want my family to be embarrassed or ashamed that I was blind. I wanted them to think that they had the best dad and husband in the world who just happened to be blind. I never wanted them to feel sorry for me, or to make them feel as if I was dependent on them for anything. I wanted to be strong, confident and independent. As much as was humanly possible, I wanted to be the same man I was before the accident.

But how was I going to accomplish this? I knew nothing about blindness. I had no idea how blind people survived from day to day, nothing about what they were capable of.

I took a major step in learning how to function as a blind man in a sighted world when I began my rehabilitation training at the Arizona Center for the Blind and Visually Impaired (ACBVI). At the center, I learned daily living skills—how to complete daily tasks around the house, how to use a white cane, how to walk with a sighted guide, and how to use adaptive computer technology. The computer technology that was available when I was trained in 1994 was pretty impressive (for its time). I learned how to use a software program called a screen-reader, which does just that. With the use of keyboard commands, it reads what is on the screen. This technology allowed me to use word pro-cessing, email, and the Internet. It literally leveled the playing field for me.

All of the technology was great, but it could not live my life for me. My first year as a blind person was brutal. Adjusting to my life with this major disability was something that I wasn't sure I could ever do. I had to learn how to do everything as a blind person. I had to learn to cook, clean, shower and shave as a blind person—and I wasn't even that good at cooking and cleaning as a sighted person.

There were many days when I felt terribly depressed. Sometimes it was one step forward and two steps back. I felt like I was a burden on my family and a burden on my wife. When I was feeling big-time sorry for myself, just about anything could bring me to tears. I seemed to constantly ~~come~~ across some relic from my 'old' life (the keys to my Porsche, a baseball glove), even a song on the radio that reminded me of a special time back when I could see. Whatever it was, it would leave me a crying mess. Kristi would try her best to make me feel better, but there was absolutely nothing she could do. To be quite honest, there were days when I just wanted to cash in my chips.

Slowly but surely, day by day, week by week, I began to accept my new life. I began to appreciate the things I could still do and the things that I still had, most notably a devoted, loving wife and twin sons. But my support group certainly didn't end there. I had an extremely compassionate extended family and many friends who stepped forward to encourage me. Unfortunately, not all my friends were up to the task of being a friend once I was unable to see. You learn who your true friends are when you go through a crisis.

After a year at home rehabilitating, I felt that I needed to get back to work. I was bored silly. I genuinely wanted to do something with my life. I knew I couldn't just sit around listening to NPR for the next forty years. I wasn't sure what I could do as a blind person, but I was determined to find out.

Fortunately, I had built my career in the property and casualty insurance business. I contacted several blind insurance agents around the country and discovered that they were operating successful agencies. This significantly buoyed my spirits. There were blind people out there leading productive, meaningful lives. So why couldn't I do it, too?

At one point, while still in college, I had seriously considered changing my major to architecture. This decision, or lack of it, came back to me now. What if I had become an architect? With the intense visual requirements of that field, it would have been impossible to return to that career. But, with insurance, there was hope.

Twelve months after losing my sight, I returned to my job as a commercial producer for a large insurance brokerage firm in Phoenix. The owners of the firm took a chance on me—something I will always appreciate. With my screen-reading computer skills, we developed an inside job. I say 'we' because they didn't know anything about hiring a blind guy. We had to create the job as we proceeded.

Those first few days back at work were both gratifying and scary. It was great to be back in the office environment, seeing old friends and colleagues. I didn't realize how much I had missed them; the conversations, the cajoling, the interactions. But it was scary, too. As I would tap my cane down the hall into different departments of the office, departments which I had confidently walked into just a year earlier, a sudden hush would permeate the space. I knew that everyone was watching me. I knew they were thinking, "How unbelievably sad. How is he ever going to be able to work?" I knew they were thinking these things—because I was thinking them, too.

But as the days turned into weeks and the weeks into months I became more confident and productive. I was able to do my work in spite of my blindness. I was proud that I was once again productive. Unless you have ever found yourself in a position where you could not work, you cannot begin to understand how much of your self-worth is defined by your career. Returning to work gave me a sense of purpose and helped me to feel that my life had meaning.

After a year of working at the brokerage, I struck out on my own. I wanted to prove (to no one but myself) that I could operate a successful insurance agency. I wanted to do the whole thing, soup to nuts. I spent the next eight years running my own shop. This was a very rewarding time for me. It was, at times, stressful, at times exhilarating, but it was never boring. I had about 100 commercial clients who kept me and my staff hopping. I took great pride in the fact that these businesses put their insurance needs in my hands, in spite of my disability. I also developed personal friendships with many of my clients.

About the same time, I returned to work, I was asked to join the board of directors of the Arizona Center for the Blind and Visually Impaired (ACBVI), the agency which had helped me learn to survive as a blind man. I was honored—and enthusiastic—about joining the board. It was a real boost to my self confidence that the agency believed in me and entrusted me to be on their board of directors to help them make decisions about governing the agency. Of course, my visits as a board member were much more invigorating and pleasant than my visits as a client had ever been. Always foremost in my mind, though, was that if I had never been a client, I probably would never have developed the skills—or confidence—to be a board member.

Very soon, after agreeing to be on the board, my motivational speaking career got off the ground. First I became a spokesman for ACBVI. It was easy, and natural. I would just tell the story of how I lost my sight and how ACBVI helped me put my life back together. One day, after I had finished a presentation to a United Way allocation meeting, I was asked to speak for the United Way campaign. I accepted, and this partnership lasted for over a decade. I met and befriended many wonderful people, both at the United Way and in many metro Phoenix businesses that were dedicated to enhancing the lives of the disadvantaged. I would probably still be speaking for them today, but the United Way changed their business model and discontinued the direct funding of social service agencies for the disabled.

One of the most important things I learned after losing my sight was to concentrate my time and effort on the things I could still do in life. I often say that before the accident there were 10,000 things I could do. Over time, I learned to focus on the 8,000 things I could still do, rather than the 2,000 I could not. Sure, I needed to do things differently, and most took me much longer to execute, but I could still do them. Changing my mindset, learning to be more patient, and being thankful for even the smallest accomplishment helped me to move forward.

Golf provided a good example of this new attitude. I was an avid golfer before losing my sight. Notice that I said 'avid'—not 'accomplished'. I had golfed since high school, and I played often. With a career in the insurance field, there was always an opportunity to hit the links, whether it was a tournament, a charity fundraiser, or just an excuse to spend time with my clients. And I certainly looked like a golfer; I had a trim, athletic build, owned sporty golf shirts, and always topped myself off with the requisite straw hat. My clubs were top notch, and everyone told me I had a very professional looking swing that was very smooth. But once the club head struck the ball, it was 'Katy, bar the door'. The ball could end up just about anywhere. I had such a huge slice, Tropicana could have sponsored me!

Not long after becoming blind, I picked up the clubs again. I had read about a number of accomplished blind golfers, and I decided to give it a shot. After some misfires of trying a few ill-fated contraptions to help me, I developed a strategy of how I could golf once again. It was awesome to return to the links.

As strange as it may sound, I am a better golfer today than I was when I could see. I know this may be difficult to believe, but my buddies tell me that my drives go 250 yards, right down the middle of the fairway. Every single one of them! I haven't been in a sand trap, lake or rough, for that matter, in twenty years. How many of you golfers can say that? A few times in every round, I out-drive the other guys in my foursome. (Actually, that part is true. Man, it feels good!)

What I have learned about golfing since becoming blind is that it is not about out-driving anyone, or whether you get a great score. It is about getting out with your buddies, enjoying the camaraderie, smelling the freshly-mown grass, warming in the sun, and simply relishing the ability to get out and golf.

One activity in which I felt sure that I was never going to participate ever again was snow skiing. Before I lost my sight, this was a sport I couldn't get enough of. I had skied all over the western United States, and I loved every minute of it—not only the skiing, but riding in the chairlifts, having lunch at the day lodge, and embracing the nightlife. I loved it all. There was a time when I spent every winter vacation on the slopes. After becoming blind, I thought this exhilarating time of my life was a thing of the past. Well...

Ten months after the accident, one of my best friends, Dino Paul, had me standing at the top of a run at North Star in Lake Tahoe—ready to ski down the slope. To say that I was scared would not even begin to scratch the surface. For our first attempt, we employed some bamboo sticks, Dino skied in front of me and I held onto them for dear life. Even though I had been an experienced skier when I was sighted, I found this new environment difficult and awkward. For our next run, we decided to ditch the bamboo sticks and use regular ski poles. Dino skied in front of me calling out the turns. Much better! Once I got used to it, I enjoyed the run; the swoosh of the skis on snow, the whoosh of the wind in my face. I was skiing! I was blind, and I was skiing! It was breathtaking!

Ski trips once again became a big part of my life. Every year, my buddies and I would head up to Park City, Utah, for a week of skiing, great food, and some fun. Even though Kristi knew it was dangerous, she still encouraged me to go. She was always a nervous wreck until I got home, but she knew that every ski trip was important to me.

Over the years, we perfected our blind guy/sighted guide team. We employed headset walkie-talkies to improve communication. Dino skied behind me and called out my turns as we traversed the slopes. Full disclosure here, I never got entirely comfortable skiing in the dark. It was a combination of pure exhilaration and sheer terror. But, for those few seconds that I was skiing down a run, I was not blind; I was invincible! As you might imagine, it was never boring. I also loved the reactions and interactions with other skiers. They often asked, "Are you really blind?" I loved it!

One of my highlights as a blind skier was beating a buddy, who will go unnamed (Brian Scott), in a NASTAR race. To this day, he will claim it never happened, but I have witnesses. The good times on the slopes and the nightlife after the sun went down were very special because I felt like I was just one of the guys.

Playing guitar was another thing that I thought I would never be able to do. I was not that great before the accident, but I figured that my lack of sight would make it virtually impossible to play at all. I had experienced a modicum of success in a rock band many years earlier. It was what would now be called classic rock, but at the time it was cutting edge stuff. I used a lot of distortion, which covered a multitude of sins.

A couple of years after losing my sight, I decided to pick up a guitar. I figured, "What the heck? How bad could it be?" To my surprise and delight, I discovered that I could still play. Like everything else in my dark world, I wasn't as proficient as I used to be. I had to learn how to do things differently. There were some things I could no longer do, but, I could still play the guitar!

Since that discovery, I have spent untold hours (and dollars!) on my new/old hobby. I play a great-sounding Heritage acoustic model and a classic Fender Telecaster. I play at family band nights, with my son Dylan (he tolerates my sloppy play) and by myself. Playing the guitar again is just another way I have been able to recreate some of the joys of my life.

In 2004, I decided to make a major change. While I enjoyed the insurance business, I felt that God had put me on this earth and helped me through a major tragedy for a bigger purpose; that telling my story could help other people who were facing challenges. So, I sold my agency and began writing my book, 'The World at My Fingertips'. I took my speaking to another level, traveling to places around the country and speaking to groups about how to overcome their own challenges.

Going back to work, serving on the ACBVI board, writing a book, and speaking were important components of my life after the accident, but they did not hold a candle to what I experienced as a husband and father. Even though I was blind, I believe that I was able to fill the role quite well.

I played Santa for the boys, snow skied with them, went to ballgames with them, taught them how to catch and throw baseballs and dribble a basketball. I believe that I did a better-than-average job as a dad. With Kristi's help, we even taught them how to ride bikes.

What I soon realized was this: the most important thing about being a dad is simply being there. I knew lots of dads who were so busy with their careers (or golfing) that they did not spend much time with their kids. Even though I could not see my boys, I dutifully went to all of their activities, including their little league baseball games, their basketball games and their Christmas plays. At least I was there, I was in the moment, and they could see me participating.

Many times I struggled during these events. Being unable to see your kids dressed in their Halloween costumes, their faces on Christmas morning, playing with the new puppy, or splashing about in the swimming pool, are moments no father should ever have to miss. During those times I had to remind myself that I was lucky to be there at all; it was a miracle that I had even survived the accident.

My marriage to Kristi has been better than I could ever have hoped or prayed for. Sure, there is lots we have wanted to do that we will never get to do. Before the accident, we dreamed of buying an RV to go on road trips across the country. That is certainly out the window now. But we can still do a lot together. We go to movies, plays, restaurants, the beach, sporting events, concerts—the list goes on and on. She is my best friend, and I think I am in her top ten.

Studies estimate that 80 to 90 percent of couples who sustain a tragedy like ours end up divorced. The ones who do survive generally have extremely strong marriages. I believe Kristi and I have a special marriage, blessed by God. As I always say, "I am a lucky man."

Steve and Kristi –
Before the storm, 1991

The obligatory eating of the wedding cake,
July 11, 1992

The wrecked Jeep, April, 1994

Kristi, in a wheelchair with our newborn twins.
May, 1994

Steve, skiing blind with Dino Paul

Kristi's Doctoral commencement, May, 2006

Chapter 1
Welker Family Update

It has been ten years since my memoir, *The World at My Fingertips,* was released. To say that a lot has happened in the past nine years would be a definite understatement. Most notably, it appears that my wife, Kristi and I have survived our twin boys' teenage years. Colton and Dylan were eleven years old when my memoir came out. They are now 21. Some times were great. Others were very challenging.

Let's start off with my wife and best friend, Dr. Kristina Welker. She is still running her successful private counseling practice in Ahwatukee. Using the gifts God bestowed her, she has helped countless people through their difficult times. She counsels couples with relationship difficulties, individuals with personal issues, and teenagers with all of the problems that come with being a teen. Given her counseling expertise (both academic and experiential), and her incredible gift of empathy, she is truly an effective counselor. In my admittedly biased opinion, I believe she has saved many marriages, careers, relationships and, yes, even lives.

As if that isn't enough, Dr. Kristina regularly writes practical advice articles for the local newspaper (Ahwatukee Foothills News), creates jewelry, and takes care of her little herd of Pomeranians. She has trained one of them, Gizmo, to be a therapy dog. Gizmo goes to work with Dr. Kristina every day. In addition to putting clients at ease, he guides them into her office and leads them to their seats, providing a moment of levity when he feels it is in order. Gizmo seems to think everyone is coming just to see him!

If Dr. Kristina ever made a mistake in her professional life, it was hiring her assistant. He misses calls, fails to notify clients of upcoming appointments, and generally performs sub-standard work. On one recent occasion, he neglected to tell a client that the office had moved. Dr. Kristina has fired him several times, but she is so kind-hearted she keeps hiring him back. The fact that he is her husband may have something to do with her patience.

But seriously... about five years ago, I started helping her with some of her administrative duties. I am good with these mundane, boring tasks, and my contribution to her work has allowed her to do more of what she is good at: counseling. It has also removed (or at least delayed) the stress of hiring an effective assistant. Plus, I work cheap. She just has to feed me once in a while. Helping her makes me feel good, too, as does anything I can do to make her life easier.

As if Kristi does not have enough on her plate, she also suffers from serious personal health issues. When people see her out in public, she is always energetic and positive; they would never know she has any ailments. But when she has a flare, she is down for the count, in bed with severe pain. It is heart-wrenching for me to be so absolutely powerless to relieve her suffering.

Kristi has Crohn's disease and fibromyalgia. She takes several different medications and she must give herself an injection once a week. Crohn's disease requires her eat an extremely limited diet. Just to name a few: no wheat, dairy, spicy foods, or alcohol. Kristi is a real trooper as she battles this condition. I don't know how she does it. To be honest, I believe that her challenges are more difficult to manage than my blindness. (I know she would disagree.) I may not be able to see, but at least I feel good every day. She awakens each morning unsure whether or not she will be able to get out of bed.

Next, an update on our boys. I'll start with Dylan. His high school years were quite uneventful—just the way parents want them to be. Dylan gave us none of the typical teenage boy challenges—smoking, drinking, drugging, girls, car wrecks, etc. Don't get me wrong, he wasn't perfect. But he was pretty close.

Dylan started playing guitar when he was eight. During high school he took his talent to a whole new level. I know I am his dad and all, but Dylan has truly turned into an amazingly, talented guitarist. He left me in the weeds when he was thirteen.

I once read that to become truly proficient at any given skill, one must spend 10,000 hours practicing. By the time Dylan was sixteen, I guesstimate that he had hit his 10,000 hours. It seems that whenever he is not driving or sleeping, that kid has a guitar in his hands. Come to think of it, I have removed a guitar from his sleeping hands on more than one occasion.

Dylan has taken this gift that God has given him and used it generously. He has played with several contemporary church bands and is currently performing at two services for Arizona Community Church. He has been on two mission trips; one to Joplin, Missouri to do cleanup work after the tornados and one to New Orleans, Louisiana to help build a home following Hurricane Katrina. Even then, after a full day of working, Dylan would strap on his guitar and join the band to play at a local church, a youth detention center, or another venue.

Dylan has also been in a couple of semi-successful rock bands; he calls his genre 'garage rock', although I am not quite sure why. To my knowledge, he has never played in a garage. 'Dylan's latest endeavor is with a band called 'Sunday at Noon'. They have released their first EP and are really quite good. But, don't take my word for it, check them out on their website at www.sundayatnoonband.com

In addition to his fledgling rock career, Dylan is attending Mesa Community College. He wants to have a back-up plan in the unlikely event that he does not become a famous musician. He is majoring in music and will soon be moving over to Arizona State University. (The 'Harvard of the Southwest', but with a better football team.)

Before I move on to Colton, I have to share our experience with the boys attaining their drivers' licenses, and then purchasing their first cars. We wanted to hold off on letting them get their drivers licenses as long as possible, knowing that only bad things could happen once they began driving. When

19

they were 17 we ran out of excuses and decided to let them get their permits.

Early on, we learned it was best to enroll the boys in a professional driving school to teach them how to drive. Initially, Kristi tried to teach them. We quickly learned this set-up made everyone in the car nervous. Trying to avoid a wreck, I thought I would give it a shot myself. If you think it sounds like a bad idea to let a blind guy teach his sons how to drive a car, you would be right. As long as they did not hit anything and no one was honking at us, I figured they were doing great. When the honking got too bad, I decided it was time to call in the professionals. It was one of the best decisions we ever made. My suggestion? Send your kid to a driving school, whether you are blind or not. It will help keep harmony in the family.

After the boys had the basics down, I thought it was important that they learn how to drive a stick shift, so we headed down to Ajo, Arizona, where my dad, Lamar, could teach them. On a bright sunny day, we drove to the abandoned Ajo airport with my dad's dune buggy. To reduce collateral damage, he drove it to the middle of the unused runway and we let them loose. Colton picked up the skill very quickly. For Dylan, it took a bit longer. My neck still hurts, thinking about all of the clutches he dumped that day. At the end of the lesson, I even jumped into the driver's seat and took the buggy for a spin. I have to admit, it felt pretty good, sitting behind a steering wheel again.

When it came time to get the boys their first cars, they continued with the trend of being as different as night and day. Colton couldn't wait for his first ride, chomping at the bit, as they say. He wanted a cool car to match his cool image. We settled on a Dodge Charger, a V-6, not the V-8 that Colton was pushing for. He immediately upgraded the stereo system and installed a sub-woofer system which took up the entire trunk (I am not joking!). Colton was very proud of this car. He washed and waxed it all the time and was very particular about how it looked. I could understand how Colton felt about his car, because that was the way I was.

As for Dylan, getting a car was very low on his priority list. He just rode along with Colton and did not see the need to have a car of his own. I could not understand this attitude. We practically had to force him to get a car. And when the big day arrived, Dylan decided on a Nissan Altima. He made this important decision with about as much enthusiasm as selecting a loaf of bread at the grocery store. For Dylan, it was just a method of getting from point A to point B. He seldom cleans the car; he sees no purpose in that. As long as he can fit his guitar and amplifiers in the car with him, he is good to go. Even though he is rather lackadaisical about it, it is a huge help, having another vehicle in the family.

Now for Colton's update. His high school years were filled with many of the trials common for that season of life. Like his father, he was not very academically motivated. Smart, yes; motivated, no. He did get very proficient at four things in high school: skateboarding, BMXing, martial arts, and video gaming. The first three things caused us to be regular guests at the local urgent care clinic.

The most dangerous of Colton's injuries was a fractured wrist, which led to avascular necrosis. This means that his wrist bone was deteriorating and could eventually require amputation of his hand. To prevent this dire consequence, Colton had to have a bone grafted from his hip, complete with the installation of metal pins. He had to use an electronic bone growth stimulator for several months. Thankfully, the surgery was successful.

Next on Colton's list of ways to create havoc, was a bike crash, in which he scraped off enough skin from his elbow to require a substantial graft. Also, during his martial arts training he dislocated his shoulder, which still bothers him today. And to top off his senior year, during his math class, Colton suffered a grand mal seizure (I think that kid would do anything to get out of doing math). As a result of the seizure, Colton's driver's license was suspended for six months, nearly a death sentence for a senior boy. Somehow, Colton managed to survive high school and graduate. After working (and partying) for a year, he got his life on track, and today he is doing great. Living independently in California, he works at a grocery store and attends Palomar College in San Marcos, where he is earning high grades. He plans to become a life coach/nutritionist/ personal trainer. Our young man is gifted with incredible communication and people skills. I have no doubt he will live the life God has planned for him.

In addition to the stresses of fatherhood, I am sure that you're sitting on the edge of your seat, wondering what else I have been up to. Well, I'm glad you asked.

I am still on the board at the Arizona Center for the Blind and Visually Impaired (ACBVI). ACBVI continues to provide recreational and rehabilitation services for the blind and is approaching its 70th year of service. A few years back, they honored me with the title of 'Chairman Emeritus'. I was truly thunderstruck, but I think it was their way of saying, "Move aside and let some younger people take over."

The Guide Dogs of the Desert in Palm Springs, California is another organization in which I have chosen to dedicate my time. Yes, I finally got a guide dog. But that's enough for now, that adventure is the subject matter of the next chapter. (In the world of professional writing, we call this a 'teaser).

In my spare time, I continue to have the same hobbies. My golf game is better than ever (Ha!) and my guitar skills continue to impress family and friends (Ha, Ha!). You will be saddened to hear that I have retired from snow skiing. While it proved to be great material for my previous book (Read it! It's funny stuff.), it was kind of a crazy thing to do. A blind guy racing down the slopes with his buddy yelling out directions was just short of lunacy. A crash into a fence post knocked some sense into my thick skull, which was, thankfully, protected by a helmet.

The Lions Club has become a big part of my life in the last few years, too. One of the group's primary focus areas is vision. The Lions were instrumental in founding both ACBVI and Guide Dogs of the Desert, and they continue to support both organizations. I suppose I got to a point at which I thought it was my duty to join a club.

My first Lions Club, the Ahwatukee Lion's, was very rewarding for me because we provided a lot of support to those in need. I ran through the chairs and enjoyed the leadership positions offered to me. After moving to Chandler, I transferred to the Chandler Lions Club. This is a very busy group that sponsors and conducts many events. It's difficult to keep track of them all. Of all of the activities that Orbit and I are involved with, there is one called 'Mistletoe Magic' that holds a special place in my heart. It is a holiday party/dinner/dance put on for special needs individuals. My Lion's club sponsors photos with Santa. Orbit has become a popular second attraction with the attendees.

Technology for the blind has improved exponentially since I wrote *The World at My Fingertips* in 2006. For the most part, developers are doing a pretty good job of making websites and software programs accessible to blind users. With screen readers, blind people can do almost anything that a sighted person can. I am writing this book on Microsoft Word™. I use Excel™ for spreadsheets and Outlook™ to correspond with my fans... and I can surf the web with the best of them.

Some sites, like Amazon and Southwest Airlines, have links specially designed for screen readers. Care to guess where I do most of my online shopping and book most of my flights?

The Arizona Talking Book Library has a digital book player available that I cannot say enough good things about. I can go to their website, download the latest books or magazines, and listen to them anywhere. I am currently listening to a new Dean Koontz book, and I can't wait to finish writing this section tonight and get back to the mayhem.

The National Federation of the Blind (NFB) has a service called News Line. Using a smartphone (or even an old-fashioned phone), users can connect and read magazines and newspapers from anywhere in the country. When I am traveling, I can keep up with all the local news—no matter where I am.

In *The World at My Fingertips*, I wrote about a brand-new service at movie theaters called audio description. This is a feature available for blind moviegoers. The blind person puts on headphones and listens to a narrator describe the on-screen action. When this technology was first offered, it often suffered from poor reception or just didn't work. Unfortunately, the visual description service was typically offered for only one movie at a time—and sometimes not at all. Well, Fortunately, this technology has rapidly progressed. At Harkins Theaters, where I go for my movie entertainment, it works almost all of the time and it is available for nearly every movie that is shown. This has made it much easier for me to keep up with what's going on. We recently saw 'American Sniper'. It would have been very difficult, if not impossible, for me to have kept up with the storyline without the audio description, even though I had read the book thanks to the Talking Book Library.

Another technological advancement is the IPhone. Apple sells this smart phone with a screen reader called voice over. This is built into each and every IPhone. It has made smart phones quite user-friendly for the blind. I wouldn't leave home without mine. I can text, check emails and the weather, surf the web, get directions, and find out how far the Earth is from the sun (just ask SIRI). These are just some of the apps that come with the phone. Additional apps I have added to my phone, allow me to take pictures of items and then describe them to me (Coke™ or Diet Coke™, chicken noodle or New England clam chowder?), read books, magazines and newspapers, check movie listings, tune my guitar, get chords for songs, listen to any radio station I want, any music I want and so much more that I would run out of room listing them all. One of the most beneficial apps I have is yoga. I can honestly say this incredible phone has made me healthier! My new favorite app is called i-grill. It has a blue tooth connection to a meat thermometer that tells me the temperature of the meat in my smoker. Pretty nifty.

Since the release of *The World at my Fingertips,* I have been blessed with much success as both an author and a motivational speaker. When people tell me that a particular section of my book has impacted them in a significant way, I am awed and humbled. When I was writing the book, I had no idea my story would touch so many people. I have completed too many book signings to count, and I have honestly enjoyed every one of them. I not only sign my name, but I add an inscription. People appreciate that a blind guy has made the effort to write them a personal note. And, I hear that most of them are legible!

For some events, I have had to sign hundreds of books in advance. You may think this unbelievably dull (not to mention the painful side-effect of getting hand cramps), but I feel quite honored to do it. The fact that people have thought enough of my story to ask me to sign their book, is a privilege I do not take lightly.

In addition, I often personally conduct motivational/ inspirational speaking events throughout the country, both for the public and for various private businesses. My presentation is called *'Radical Resiliency: The awe-inspiring ability to overcome challenges and lead an extraordinary life'*.

Most people have to pay to attend my sessions, or book a counseling appointment with Dr. Kristina, but in this book we will share the skills that you need to bounce back from any adversity. So, keep reading and discover your own radical resiliency!

Family – Thanksgiving, 2014

Dylan onstage with 'Sunday at Noon' Pub Rock,
Scottsdale, October, 2015

Colton at home in San Diego, summer, 2015

Steve speaking to Henkel Dial Corporation –
Scottsdale, AZ, 2009

Chapter 2
Orbit Joins The Family

O ver the years, I occasionally considered getting a guide dog. I am a dog lover, so increasingly I would think about how much help a dog could provide, not to mention how cool it would be. But I knew it would represent a big commitment. I would be required to train at the guide dog school for several weeks, and then it would become a long-term relationship.

In 2012, my mindset changed. That was the year our sons, Colton and Dylan, graduated from high school. I had often joked that my two-legged guides were moving on and it was time to get a four-legged one. When the joke turned into a real need, I sent in an application to the Guide Dogs of the Desert organization located in Palm Springs, California.

I requested a standard poodle, which would almost certainly take longer than the four-to-six-month wait to get a more popular breed like a German shepherd or a Labrador retriever. I wanted a poodle for a couple of reasons. They are hypoallergenic and do not shed. After all, I spend a good deal of time in other people's cars, homes and offices; I didn't like the idea of my dog leaving a hairy calling card everywhere we went.

I had never been around standard poodles and I didn't know much about them. Then, as fate would have it, the Arizona Center for the Blind and Visually Impaired hosted a fundraiser with the members of The Guide Dogs of the Desert. At that event, I was able to spend some time with these cool dogs. I was impressed at how poised and proud they stood. The word 'regal' came to mind. I was sold. I had to have one.

After a two-year wait, I finally got the call. In March of 2014, I received a phone call and was told that my 'tall' poodle was ready. That is all they would reveal. They wouldn't even tell me the gender. I was to report to the training facility in late April, and, contrary to what I believed, the training was to last a month, not two weeks. Well, I thought I was much too busy and important to just take off for what seemed like a very long time. As it turned out, though, I wasn't nearly as important or as busy as I had believed.

Beginning on April 28, 2014, I began four very full weeks at the Guide Dogs of the Desert facility in White Water, California, just outside Palm Springs. Truth is, the timing turned out to be less than perfect. We had just moved into a brand new home in Chandler, Arizona, and Kristi was scheduled to move into a new office on May 1. I hated to leave her to deal with all of the projects associated with settling into a new home and a new office, but I had no choice. Doesn't it seem that this is the way life happens? You go along for several months (or even years) and everything is relatively calm. Then, it seems as though several big changes come down the pike—all at the same time. As they say, "When it rains, it pours!"

So much for the thought that four weeks would be overkill! Actually, I was glad for every single day—both for the training, (mostly training me) and for the incredible bonding that developed between my new dog and me. For the first two-and-a-half days, the trainers familiarized us with our guide dog gear and taught us the basic commands and obedience principles that apply specifically to guide dogs. Then, for the entire morning of day three, we spent time pretending to be guided by a stuffed dog (read: trainer pushing around a stuffed dog).

Finally, on the afternoon of the third day, April 30, we got our dogs. I couldn't believe how excited I became in the moments just before I was to meet my new companion. I felt like a kid on Christmas morning. His name is Orbit. He is a tall, blue standard poodle with silver markings. I immediately fell in love with this big boy.

Later that day, it hit me. The date, April 30, was the 20th anniversary of the accident that took my sight. In a spiritually significant way, the very same day that I lost my sight was the day—two decades later—that I got my sight back—via my new, four-legged helper.

I had frequently heard that poodles were rather standoffish, but you couldn't prove it by Orbit. From the moment they handed me his leash, it was as if he knew he had been specially bred, raised and trained just for me. He leaned into me and soaked up all of the attention we were getting from everyone. We then went off to my (no, our) room to get to know each other.

The dorm room was fairly small, and Orbit immediately hopped up on the bed. I could picture him curling up on my bed, looking around, and thinking, 'Hey, this training shouldn't be too bad. This is much nicer than the kennel and all of those stinky, noisy Labrador retrievers and German shepherds. I quickly showed Orbit his own bed and explained that was where he was to sleep. He understood the arrangements immediately, and we didn't have any more sleeping issues.

The four weeks of training was not so much exhausting as it was intense. We were up every morning at 6:00 to feed and relieve our dogs; then off to breakfast at 7:00. The training day consisted of learning to walk with our new guides at parks, malls, train stations, etc. We would work until about 4:00, then feed the dogs again. Final relieving was at 8:30. Then Orbit and I would crash on our respective beds.

They have a saying at the school, "It's a lot of work, but it's worth it!" Today I can report that there's nothing but truth in that little homily.

I can't say enough about how impressed I was with the staff and the trainers at Guide Dogs of the Desert. They treated each one of us like VIPs. They took care of our every need—meals, lodging and pretty much anything else that we needed. Don't get me wrong; it wasn't the Ritz. But we weren't there for a vacation—we were there for training. They were called dorms, after all.

And did I mention the cost? I may have forgotten—because there was no cost to the students. That's right. These amazing dogs, the training, the lodging, the meals, the transportation, and even the date milkshakes were all provided to the students free of charge.

Most people could never afford to buy one of these dogs. I was told that each assigned dog that leaves this non-profit school with a new best friend, has over $50,000 invested in it. The dollar cost includes an in-house breeding program, puppy raising, and guide dog training.

Through the generosity of many sources, including individual donors, foundations, corporate donations, Lion's Clubs and other service organizations, the school is able to provide this life- changing service to the blind at no cost.

For the first few days of training with our 'real' dogs, we just walked around the campus. It was mostly walking to and from the dining room. As these were routes I had already trekked several times with my white cane, I didn't fully realize or appreciate the fact that Orbit was guiding me. But that was about to change.

Our first 'real-world' walk involved a drive to the American Legion Hall in Palm Springs. The trainers herded us into the building. Then, one team at a time, they took us outside for walks. This may not seem like a big deal, but I was nervous. Was I really going to let a dog walk me around the streets of Palm Springs? Before I could get too anxious, it was Orbit's turn... my turn!

Out the door, then a quick left... and there we were, walking down the sidewalk with a trainer. For the first twenty-five steps or so, I was more than a little uncomfortable. No white cane, no sighted guide. Just my left hand on a handle. I was relying 100% on this dog to guide me safely along the route. It wasn't long before it occurred to me that Orbit knew exactly what he was doing. I was the rookie here. So I relaxed (slightly) and tried to enjoy the walk. After the next twenty-five steps, I started to think, "Hey. This might actually work!" I'm not sure, but I may have said that aloud.

At the beginning of our training, head trainer Bob Wendler, told me that standard poodles were very different from any other breed of guide dog he had ever worked with. He explained that they are multitaskers. Other breeds, such as Labradors, pretty much just put their heads down and go about their business; Poodles, keep their heads up and are constantly looking to see what is going on around them. When he first started training poodles, Bob said, he thought they would never work out. Initially, he believed that they might be too easily distracted. What he discovered, though, was that they were actually just taking everything in. In spite of the fact that they were constantly looking around, they remained diligently on task.

I soon discovered that Orbit—still in training, of course—could stray from the straight and narrow from time to time. Here's what happened a couple of weeks into the course.

Guide dogs are trained to notify their blind handler of a step or curb by stopping at the change in elevation. The handler will then probe with his left foot to find the step, then tell the dog to go forward. And so it was with us: Orbit and me. We were working the dogs at an outdoor mall on a warm, breezy day in May. I was quite relaxed by now, pretty much free to depend on Orbit. Unfortunately, he blew down a couple of steps without stopping to notify me. I was able to catch myself before I did a face plant, but it was quite a surprise.

As a result of this problem, Bob wanted us to work a bit more on steps to help correct the mistake. He went to the top of a long flight of stairs while Orbit and I waited below. Following Bob's direction, Orbit and I started for the stairs. As usual, Orbit's head seemed to be on a swivel, looking back and forth. As we approached the bottom of the stairs, Orbit suddenly veered to the left and I felt myself walking up a long ramp. The next thing I heard was Bob, laughing. Upon approaching the stairs, Orbit had found a better way to get me up to Bob; a ramp that ran along the side of the stairs. Bob decided that no correction was in order, since Orbit had simply found the safest, easiest way to get me from point A to point B. Today, Orbit nearly-always does a great job of notifying me of steps.

A common misperception about blind people is that all of us are totally blind. In fact, most people identified as blind have some residual vision. Unfortunately, I have virtually no vision. Strange enough, this caused a slight problem in my training. There are only a few basic commands a handler gives his dog; forward, halt, left, right, and 'get busy'. (I'll let you guess what that last one means). The dogs are trained to take their handlers from point A to point B, as directed by the handler. As the handler and dog become more in 'sync' with each other and certain trends repeat themselves, the dog will develop the ability to intuit what the owner wants. Because I am totally blind, there was no way for me to determine just when it was time to tell Orbit to turn. For example, a visually impaired person could make out an intersecting sidewalk. I could not. I loved how Bob resolved this problem. "Fake it", he told me. I had to laugh. However, I must say, I have mastered this technique. I just wait until I feel Orbit start to turn. I can feel his movements through my grip on his harness handle. Then I tell him to turn in that direction, and he completes the turn. I am not sure whether I am fooling Orbit or Orbit is fooling me, but it works.

On the morning of our last day of training, the trainers took us to Walmart and cut us loose. We were finally allowed to walk alone with our dogs. Orbit and I walked around for thirty minutes, down the grocery aisles, into the auto section, out to the garden area, into the beauty shop (don't ask me, I was letting Orbit guide me!), all over the store. Who knew that walking around a Walmart could be so exhilarating? It was the first time I had walked by myself without a white cane or sighted guide in over twenty years. I probably would have cried, if I wasn't having so much fun.

These days, Orbit is my sidekick all the time. We are rarely apart. His dedication to me is truly awesome. If he goes outside and someone else lets him in, he will search the house until he finds me. If I leave the house for any amount of time, he gets so excited at my return that you would think I had been gone for days. He is my constant companion, friend and guide. As a matter of fact, he is sitting on the floor next to me as I write this (making editorial comments). It is really heartwarming to see his dedication. It is as if he is saying, "Do you need my help, daddy? Do you need me to guide you anywhere?" Detractors say that using dogs as guides is abusive. I believe the opposite is the case. Orbit loves to work; he loves to be needed. Whenever I walk down the hall to get his harness off the hook, his tail starts wagging. Then he is all business; his demeanor changes and he becomes more than a dog—he knows he is a guide dog, and he enjoys the work.

At the end of the class, a graduation ceremony was held. It was a big deal. Hundreds of people (and dogs) showed up. Puppy raisers, sponsors, trainers, family and friends attended.

Kristi and Dylan drove to Palm Springs for the big day. I wasn't worried about how Kristi and Orbit would get along, but I was curious. Kristi is a dog lover, but Pomeranians are her favorite breed. Her dogs are very small, and Orbit is very big. As expected, the meeting went great. Kristi immediately fell in love with Orbit—and Orbit with her. For a month I had been regaling her with our adventures. She already understood and appreciated the independence I had gained from having Orbit, and for that alone she instantly loved him. As for Orbit, it was as if he already knew that Kristi played an important role in my life. He is still absolutely devoted to me, but they have become great friends.

I wasn't sure what to expect from Orbit when we got home and he was not working. I figured he would just lie around until I needed him. While he does his fair share of napping, he also loves to play like a big puppy. He throws his toys around the house, plays chase with us, and tries to get the other dogs to play with him. (Although, he is ten times their size and they are mostly terrified of him).

Barbara Norman and Alan Franks, who raised Orbit from his birth, were not surprised when we told them about his antics. They had nicknamed him 'Goofy'. The nickname has stuck.

And speaking of people who raise these fantastic puppies, let me take a moment to thank all puppy raisers. Without your selfless dedication there would be no service dogs. In Orbit's case, Barbara and Alan spent two years with this young dog, teaching him basic obedience and how to behave in public. They took care of him; feeding, grooming and when needed, took him to the vet. Then, when he was old enough and had cleared all of the hurdles, they returned him to the Guide Dogs of the Desert for more training. These are special people. I can tell you right now, I would not be able to do what they do.

Orbit's training was not yet complete. Think of the puppy-raising phase as the equivalent of, in human terms, elementary and high school. Learning to be a guide dog, is more like college. For his degree in guide 'dog-ology', Orbit spent six months with two gifted professors at Guide Dogs of the Desert, Michal Anna Padilla and Emily Goodland. They taught him everything he needed to know in order to safely guide me around any obstacle that we might encounter in on our daily travels. Every day I come home in one piece, I have these skilled trainers to thank.

One of the main lessons the trainers kept drilling into our heads was: listen to your dog! By this they meant that even if the dog is doing—or not doing—something you want him to do, listen to him (your knucklehead!). He can see and is trained, while you can't—and aren't.

I received a great example of this soon after Orbit and I returned home. One day, we were out on a walk, taking a path we had traversed several times. When we approached the front of our house, Orbit suddenly stopped dead in his tracks. Having no idea why he stopped, I commanded, "Forward." He took one step and stopped again. Becoming frustrated, I sternly told him, "Forward". He took one step and stopped again. I was seriously considering whether I should call the school and tell them that Orbit needed some more training, but I decided to listen to my dog. I probed in front of me and, sure enough, there was a huge obstacle. A pallet of sod, for our front yard, was stacked on the sidewalk. I praised Orbit profusely while simultaneously chiding myself, "Listen to your dog, you knucklehead!" The lesson was not yet complete. I told Orbit to "go right" so we could step down onto the street and go around the pallet. But I got the same response from my canine guide. One step, then he stopped. Starting to learn my lesson, I probed the street with my foot, immediately kicking a four-foot high pallet of pavers. I directed Orbit to go into the yard and around the obstacles, repeating to myself, "Listen to your dog Steve! Listen to your dog!"

Within a month of returning home with my new best friend, it was time to get to work. I had a speaking engagement at Assurance America, an insurance company in Atlanta, Georgia. There were lots of firsts—first solo trip with Orbit, first speech with Orbit, and first airline flight with Orbit. And it was Orbit's first flight ever! Even though he had been through two and a half years of extensive training, my guide dog had never been on an airplane. I was a bit anxious. It was a four-hour flight to Atlanta. How would he handle the crowds at the airport? How would he behave on the plane? As it turned out, I needn't have wasted my energy worrying.

At the terminal, my super-dog was in full control. I practically had to run to keep up with him. It was the first time I experienced his impersonation of Moses parting the Red Sea. He just got into the middle of the concourse and cruised. I could literally hear fellow travelers scampering out of our way.

On the plane, Orbit just couldn't have behaved any better. Fortunately, we were sitting in the first row of first class. My companion had plenty of room to stretch out and sleep, and, for most of the long flight, that's exactly what he did. At the end of the flight, the attendants complimented him, telling me he behaved better than some of their human passengers. The first class cabin attendant also shared with me that some passengers were now bringing their pets on flights, claiming they were emotional support animals. They were clearly untrained, jumping onto empty seats and running around the cabin. She told me it was clear that Orbit was a highly trained service animal. It was a nice end to my new friend's first flight.

After we landed, we were off to an Atlanta Braves baseball game, another first for Orbit. It was crowded, hot, and horribly muggy. As I had come to expect from my new assistant, his guiding was great and his behavior was exemplary. Our three days in Atlanta were outstanding, and I discovered a level of freedom and independence while traveling that I had not experienced since our accident.

These days, Orbit is a constant companion whenever I travel. At school, they told us that the guide dogs would be able to lay down at the foot area in front of the seat. I tried this once with my big boy. Not a chance! He tried, being the trooper he is, but he is just too tall. So, when we travel, I make sure we are sitting in the first row, behind the bulkhead. I just have to hope that the passenger sitting next to me is a dog lover. So far, so good.

Unfortunately, life hasn't totally been 'flying the friendly skies' since I received Orbit. At a recent church picnic, we experienced a terrifying situation that reminded us of how careful we have to be when we are out with my service dog.

Orbit and I were walking down a sidewalk, minding our own business. Suddenly, and without warning, a dog that was part pit bull, attacked Orbit from the rear. The dog was vicious and with teeth bared, tried over and over again to bite Orbit on the neck.

Guide dogs are trained to be very docile. This is imperative for a couple of reasons. First, a service dog needs to be very well mannered to insure proper behavior when out in public. Second, a calm dog helps to limit the duration of a dogfight, thus reducing injuries. If the aggressive dog feels that he has 'won, the battle' he is more likely to break off the fight.

True to his training, Orbit tried to get down on the ground in front of me so he would minimize his potential injuries from the attack and to protect me. That move, combined with Kristi and me yelling at the aggressive dog, finally got the dog to back off. Thankfully, Orbit sustained only minor injuries.

Our biggest concern was Orbit's psychological state. How would being attacked by another dog affect his performance as a guide dog? Immediately after the incident, he appeared to be on high alert, looking out for another attack. With time, Orbit is now doing much better. Still, he is not comfortable when we are out and he sees other dogs. As time passes, I hope he will become less vigilant. If not, I may need to send him back to guide dog school for some correctional training.

Personally, I do not understand why people own vicious dogs. I have read that pit bulls make up only 6% of the dog population but are responsible for over 60% of dog attacks. In general, I believe that vicious dogs should not be out in public.

In Orbit's case, the dog was on leash, but its handler was incapable of firmly holding onto it. So, the dog pulled away and took off. If you own one of these potentially aggressive dogs, please, please, please make sure the dog is safely secured. If you need more motivation, be aware that it is a violation of the Americans with Disabilities Act (ADA) to injure a service animal, thus making it a federal offense. In addition, the owner of an attacking dog would be held liable for any damages. To put a dollar amount on it, Orbit is worth over $50,000. So if you don't want to pay a large fine or face possible jail time, then keep your dog under control. Service animals are not just pets; they serve as an important lifeline for their handlers.

Vicious dogs aside, walking today is a very different experience from what it was before I had Orbit. When I have his handle in my hand, I am much more confident, so much more independent. Kristi says that I literally stand taller, confidently pushing my shoulders back. When Orbit and I are cruising, I am oblivious to most of the obstacles we walk past. When using a white cane, I had to touch an obstacle with the cane to determine where I was. A curb, a rock, a wall, a car—I had to tap it with my cane to know that it existed so I could move around it. Orbit simply maneuvers me through the obstacle course; I am just along for the ride. The expression 'Whistling through the graveyard' comes to mind.

I appreciate every sighted guide who has ever helped me, but they have done just that; helped me. Since I became blind, it has been my goal to be independent and to rely on others only if it is absolutely necessary. The great thing about having a guide dog is, I am no longer dependent on anyone. Now I can walk around by myself. Unless you are disabled, you cannot know how invigorating it is to find independence.

When I am in public with Orbit, he is the center of attention. At the mall, at a ballgame, navigating through the airport terminal, or at the beach, people always want to know all about him. Where did I get him? What does he do for me? How long was he in training? What kind of dog is he? Can he tell red lights from green lights? (The answer to that last question is 'no').

I never tire of the inquiries. Orbit and I (and whomever we are with) are ambassadors for guide dogs. It is important for everyone to understand what these service animals are capable of, and how they benefit the blind. Some people I have met show interest in becoming puppy raisers, getting guide dogs for themselves or for loved ones or supporting the cause. I love my new guide dog ambassador job!

When I am with Orbit, I am often asked if it is OK to pet him. This is a slippery slope, because each owner feels differently about this topic. Some do not want anyone to pet or talk to their dogs at any time. Others will allow people to pet them when they are not working. (The dog is working when the owner has the harness, or handle, in his hand. If the owner has the leash in his hand, the dog is not working.)

When the dog is working, his single focus should be to get the owner from point A to point B as safely as possible. Distractions—such as people who want to pet the dog—interfere with this task. If someone comes up to the dog and starts petting him, the guide dog will stop being a guide dog and start being a pet.

I love the fact that people are so interested in him, and it is sometimes difficult for us to ignore them and keep on trucking, but it is what both Orbit and I need to do. For example, when I am at the mall, if I stop to let everyone pet Orbit, it would take me all afternoon to get my shopping done. So, if you see us out and about and you think we are being rude, please know we are just focusing on the task at hand; safely getting from one place to another.

When our training sessions in Palm Springs were almost over, head trainer Bob Wendler took us on a night walk to a fountain called 'the rainmaker'. (I wanted to tell Bob they were all night walks for me, but I decided he probably knew that). The fountain consists of canisters that slowly fill with water; when they got to a tipping point, gravity took over and the canisters dumped their contents into the larger pool. As I listened to the water cascading downward, I thought, "This is like memories in a person's life. Each canister represents a different stage—youth, college, adulthood, marriage, parenthood and retirement. When you complete each season of life, all those memories pour into the memory pool of life and you start a new phase, a new chapter, and a new season."

I started filling a new canister of memories when I became blind on April 30, 1994. The day I got Orbit, April 30, 2014, all of those recollections poured into my life's memory pool and I started filling a new memory canister. Orbit has been by my side nearly every minute of every day since I got him. He has changed my life and made this new canister more interesting and more enjoyable than any in the two decades before he came. His presence and his power have made me more independent and freer than I could have ever imagined.

Steve, Kristi and Orbit at Carlsbad beach,
summer, 2014

Steve and Orbit out for a walk,
Chandler, AZ, summer, 2015

Orbit at his first Diamondbacks game
Phoenix, AZ, summer, 2014

Steve, Kristi and Orbit after presentation at
Guide Dogs of the Desert, Spencer's Restaurant,
Palm Springs, CA, November, 2014

Chapter 3
What Is Radical Resiliency?

Interest in resiliency has grown tremendously in the past couple of decades. Much has been written, researched and reviewed regarding depression, anxiety and post-traumatic stress disorder. However, psychologists often tend to look at 'what's wrong' with people instead of embracing 'what's right'. Rather than focusing on what makes people sick, the most important answers may lie in understanding how and why people stay well.

Why do some people persevere? What allows some people to face adversity with panache? What separates those who emotionally thrive and those whose spirit withers and dies? We are about to examine the negative effects of stress—and the therapeutic modalities that enable individuals to become resilient.

It is now well established that protective psychological factors are needed to prevent illness. As a matter of fact, it is estimated that 75 to 80% of all doctor's visits are precipitated by stress. The good news is that individuals who struggle with depression, anxiety, illness or trauma can now learn how to successfully overcome their distress by focusing on the characteristics that resilient people adhere to during times of stress.

Dr. Janoff-Bulman, who is a pioneer of resiliency research states, "If inner core beliefs can be restored to some degree, if individuals can rebound from extremely hurtful events, they may be better able to cope with future painful experiences." When people acquire the tools to effectively overcome trauma, they are much better at dealing with trauma the second or third time around.

This book intends to shed light on how individuals can face adversity effectively and how to meet crises 'head on'—in order to thrive and prosper in spite of them.

ઇ

Life is all about change. Regardless of your station in life: your age, your financial status, or any other measuring stick that you wish to use, you are continually going through changes of one kind or another. I believe that there are three different types of changes:
   • Intentional Change
   • Unintentional Change
   • External Change
Let's look briefly at each one.

Intentional changes are changes that you make by conscious decision. They are generally positive changes, moving you toward becoming the person you want to be. They include major life decisions such as:
   • going to college
   • choosing a career
   • deciding where to live
   • getting married
   • starting a family
   • pursuing hobbies
   • committing to an exercise program
   • starting a diet
Hopefully, you devote a good deal of time and energy in making these decisions. *Unintentional changes* can sneak up on you and manifest themselves in your life by unconscious decisions or by default. These are not changes that you plan on. As you can imagine, they are usually negative.

Your health—mental or physical—is a good example.
   • choosing to forgo exercise
   • getting inadequate sleep
   • failing to stick to a healthy eating program.

All of these cause unintended negative changes. Other examples of unintentional changes include staying at an unfulfilling job, or in a toxic relationship.

Often the reason individuals remain in negative situations is that it takes time and effort to make a change, and making a change can be terrifying. Oftentimes, people have to get to a boiling point before they finally decide to make the changes that they need to make.

External changes are those in which you have no control. They can be *negative* or *positive*. *Negative* external changes may include events or conditions such as:

- a poor economy
- a natural disaster
- an illness
- an accident
- the loss of a loved one.

On the other hand, *Positive* external changes, include wonderful gifts such as receiving an inheritance or profiting from a healthy economy.

The key for living a happy, fulfilling life is to decide how you will manage change. The more goals you set—by writing them on your intentional change checklist and completing that list—the happier your life will be.

Conversely, the more situations that pop up on your *unintentional change* list, the less satisfied you will be. Successfully removing items from the *unintentional change* category and moving items into the *intentional change* category (by changing an attitude or a behavior—or both) will govern the state of your health and well-being. How you handle external changes, both negative and positive, will also factor into your happiness quotient.

Resilient people have mastered change and the art of moving through it. They have discovered the power of 'Radical Resiliency.'

So, just what is radical resiliency? It is the awe-inspiring ability to overcome challenges and lead an extraordinary life. In my workshops, I teach people how to develop these skills, not only to survive, but to thrive.

I am often asked how I was able to put my life back together after I suffered a traumatic brain injury (TBI) and lost my eyesight. People often imply that I must have superhuman powers to have overcome such a traumatic experience. Nothing could be further from the truth.

I was an average guy, with average hopes and aspirations, who was very happy cruising through a rather comfortable life when, unfortunately, the wheels came off. At that juncture I had two choices: I could either fall into a deep-pit-of depression (and believe me, there were many times that I wanted to do just that), or I could embrace what I could still do and make the best of it.

Over time, I figured out that I could still accomplish 80% of the things I could do prior to the auto accident that took my sight. True, I have to do most things in a different way—and it may take me longer to do—but I can still complete the task. So, which would I rather focus on- the 20% of the things that I cannot do, or the 80% of the things that I still can?

"Do not let what you cannot do
interfere with what you can do."
~ John Wooden

With the help of Kristi, my family and friends, and the Lord, I have been able to focus on the positive. I have been able to live what I consider to be an extraordinary life. I would even argue that I am living a more rewarding, fulfilling life than I was living before I lost my sight.

"As he passed by, he saw a man blind from birth.
And his disciples asked him,
"Rabbi, who sinned, this man or his parents,
that he was born blind?"
Jesus answered, "It was not that this man sinned,
or his parents,
but that the works of God might be displayed in him."
~ John 9:1-3

The obvious question is this. How can a person be resilient? Are these skills hard-wired from birth? Are they only available to the super strong? The super wealthy? The super lucky? The answer is: NO! The good news is that these skills can be developed before, during or after a crisis. Why wait? You can start building resiliency skills now.

Studies show that more than two-thirds of all individuals lack basic resiliency skills that are needed to overcome adversity. But don't panic! The reason you don't have these skills is that you probably never needed them. But what if you begin building those skills immediately so you are ready for any curve-balls that life may throw at you? If life's difficulties buck you off the horse, no problem. Just dust yourself off, mount the horse, and get back in the race.

The Resiliency Triangle

Each of us probably knows at least one person who has been dealt blow after blow, but they continue to get up and move on. What makes these people so strong? How are they able to deal with one crisis after another? There are three primary characteristics that resilient people possess. We define them as 'The Resiliency Triangle'.

- Positive Attitude
- Commitment to Accomplishing Goals
- Strong Support System

Next, we will drill down into these three vital elements to show you how to create your own Resiliency Triangle.

"I have learned that success is to be measured
not so much by the position that one has reached in life as by the
obstacles overcome while trying to succeed."
~ Booker T. Washington

Chapter 4
The Resiliency Triangle–
Positive Attitude

"A joyful heart is good medicine,
but a crushed spirit dries up the bones."
~ Proverbs 17:22

Resilient people have positive attitudes. This may sound trite, but I believe it is the most critical resiliency skill. I am not talking about a Pollyanna, over the top optimistic person who seems to be a bit too exuberant—all the time and in any circumstance. The Flanders character from The Simpsons comes to mind. No, I believe that a positive attitude is merely the ability to look at any situation in the best possible light, instead of the worst.

Let's take a look at some facts about attitude.

You are not born with a positive or negative attitude

Psychologists have discovered that your attitude is not determined at birth. Individual attitudes are acquired from your life experiences. Some people say, "I can't help it. I was born with a negative disposition." This simply is not the case.

"Most folks are as happy as they make up their minds to be."
~ Abraham Lincoln

"Nothing can stop the man with the right mental attitude from achieving his goals, nothing on earth can help the man with the wrong mental attitude."
~ Thomas Jefferson

I wholeheartedly agree with the sentiments of these two great American presidents. At one time or another, all of us have decided how we will react to a situation. The fact that we can control our attitude tells us that we choose whether we will react positively or negatively. Thoughts are random, feelings are a choice,

Replace negative thoughts with positive ones

Resilient people have the ability to replace damaging, negative thoughts with positive thoughts. This may sound like it would be easy to do, but it takes time to do it. Your brain must be trained. The main problem with thinking negatively is that it causes a downward spiral, which can end up leaving you very depressed. Once there, it can take a Herculean effort to climb out of the miserable mood. Fortunately, you can train your brain to immediately replace those negative thoughts with positive thoughts as soon as they pop into your brain. It takes a conscious, intentional effort on your part. As soon as the negative thought or emotion starts to creep in, define what you are feeling. Give yourself permission to feel what you feel. Then re-direct your negative thought to a positive thought. Take action. Go on a walk. Listen to music. Read a book. Call a friend.

> "Your mind can only hold one thought at a time,
> make it a positive, constructive one."
> ~ H. Jackson Brown, Jr.

After I became blind, I found it extremely difficult to erase negative thoughts. Just about any occasion would cause me to think about how horrible it was to be blind. Once I started down the rabbit hole, I could waste a whole day, or even several days, in a state of self-inflicted sadness. Over the years, as I became aware of this negative thought process, I developed the ability to sense it coming on. I would then make the conscious decision to cancel that thought and start thinking about something else, something positive. Let me give you a couple of examples.

When the boys were about ten years old, the family was preparing to go to a Phoenix Suns game and we needed to program the car's GPS. I backed the car out of the garage so we could connect to the satellite. Dylan casually hopped into the passenger seat. No big deal, right? Wrong! This was the first time this scenario had ever taken place; me in the driver's seat, my son in the passenger's seat. If I hadn't been blind, this simple event of me driving with my son would have occurred several times a day. But it was an occurrence that we would never experience together.

This simple incident nearly brought me to tears. I had always been a guy who loved to drive. I had eagerly anticipated driving my family to sporting events, church, road trips, and heck, even the grocery store. But now I would never be able to drive my family anywhere, except out of the garage. As I contemplated my sad state of affairs, Dylan noticed.

"Are you OK, dad?" he innocently asked. I had to make a decision. Should I tell him what I had been thinking, or mentally cancel that negative thought and get back to the task of programming the navigator? I decided on the latter. I was able to see that by being negative I could easily spoil this fun evening that we had planned. We programmed the navigator. Kristi drove us to the game. We successfully found the arena— and had a great time.

Another example of replacing negative thoughts with positive ones transpired when we went to a car dealership to purchase Colton's first car. After completing all of the required paperwork, we walked from the sales office and across the showroom, ostensibly to pick up the car, a bright red Dodge Charger. I recall thinking, "There it is, just outside the showroom, all ready for my son." That's when the enormity of my loss hit me like a ton of bricks. "This is not fair," I thought. "My son is picking up his first car and I can't see it. I can't witness the excitement in his face. I can't appreciate what his new car looks like. This is really not fair!"

I almost began crying right then and there; I had to choke back the tears. I knew that if I broke down visibly I would ruin this special occasion for my entire family. (And, believe me, there were plenty of times I did just that). But on this occasion I was able to replace the extremely negative thoughts with positive ones in a matter of seconds. "Get a grip," I told myself. "You're lucky to be here at all. Your car accident could just as easily have killed you. You could be buried under a headstone with your name and two dates on it. Be thankful for what you have!" I took a deep breath and did an immediate 180° mental turnaround. My family had no idea that I had nearly 'lost it.'

I realized that I could hear and feel Colton's excitement. We walked around the car to check it out. After giving it the 'good to go', I climbed into the passenger seat and we drove home. It was just a son taking his dad on a maiden voyage with his new car. What could be more normal than that?

Keep busy

Another key to avoiding negative thoughts is to keep busy. There is an old saying: 'An idle mind is the devil's workshop.' In this case, the devil is in those negative thoughts. The longer you sit around doing nothing, the more opportunity the devil has to come in and do his work.

In those early days, to keep my mind off of the fact that I could not see, I tried to find activities that I could do in the house. Anything was better than sitting around feeling sorry for myself. I rode the exercise bike, read books, played the guitar, and went for walks... just to keep my mind busy. While this did not work 100% of the time, I am sure that my trips 'down the rabbit hole' were significantly reduced.

You will read more about negative thinking in Chapter 9, *Stomp Out Negative Thinking.*

Find the silver lining

Another key feature of resilient people is their ability to find the silver lining behind the dark clouds. Life really is like the weather. Most of us have down days. Not every day can be sunny. 'Into every life a little rain must fall.' The question is: how do you handle those days when the sun isn't shining?

I am sure you know at least one person who sees only the dark clouds and never notices the silver lining. You have probably observed that whenever you are around that person, you find yourself drawn into their oppressive mood. It is important to limit the time you spend with people who bring you down. It is difficult to fly like an eagle when turkeys surround you. Make sure you are not one of the turkeys. Here is a story that exemplifies that theory.

A shoe manufacturing company in the United States decided to expand its territory in an underdeveloped country in South America. In order to do so, they sent two investigators to see if this would be a profitable venture. One of the investigators was a turkey; he always focused on the negative. The other investigator was an eagle; he always saw the silver lining.

A month later, the investigators entered the home office, ready to report their discoveries. The turkey slouched up to the head of the conference.

"I am sorry to report," he glumly said, "There is no viable market for a shoe manufacturing plant in this poor country. No one down there wears shoes."

The turkey then dropped his head and slouched back into his seat. Those in attendance believed that this proposition might be a lost cause.

The eagle then stood, pulled his shoulders back, confidently approached the microphone and smiled broadly. "I disagree" he stated. "I think the potential is unlimited. *No one down there has shoes.*"

Both investigators witnessed the same conditions; no one in the country wore shoes. However, the turkey saw this as a roadblock; the eagle saw it as a huge opportunity. Acting on the eagle's recommendation, the shoe manufacturing plant was built—and the company made millions.

So, who do you want to be, the turkey or the eagle? The choice is yours. Just look for the silver lining.

"...but those who hope in the LORD
will renew their strength.
They will soar on wings like eagles;
they will run and not grow weary,
they will walk and not be faint."

~ Isaiah 40:31

Maintain a sense of humor

When faced with difficult situations, a good sense of humor is imperative. Many people say that laughter is the best medicine. Well, I say that medicine is the best medicine, but laughter is a close second.

You may be thinking that you are not a funny person. Understand, I am not talking about slapping-your-knee-and-snorting funny. I am talking about being able to see the lighter side. Sometimes, things get so ridiculous that you just have to laugh.

Kristi and I ran into this a few months after I returned home from the hospital. It was an extremely difficult time for us. I was learning how to live as a blind person (and having a rather difficult time of it). We were both healing from our injuries, physically and mentally. And we had babies, so we were not getting much sleep. We felt like we were up against impossible odds. We were holding on for dear life.

As a result of the accident, I lost my right eye, which was replaced with a prosthetic eye. Contrary to popular belief, a prosthetic eye is not a glass eye. It is neither glass nor round. It is made of acrylic and is shaped like a thick contact lens. An 'eye' is painted onto the surface to resemble a real eye. The acrylic eye must be cleaned on a regular basis.

In those early days, I could not take out the prosthetic, so Kristi had to do it for me (talk about true love). One afternoon, as I lay on the bed, she used a small suction cup to remove the eye. As I lay there, I heard her at the sink, rinsing it. Then I heard her walk to the towel rack, which hung over the toilet, to dry it. I am sure you have figured out what happened next. Splash! That's right. She dropped the eye into the toilet.

There were a few moments of embarrassed silence, and then I started laughing. What else could I do? This was such a ridiculous situation! My wife had just dropped my eye into the toilet. Six months earlier, I could not have imagined that scenario. Kristi ran over to me. She was worried that I was crying. When she saw I was laughing, she was confused.

"What's so funny?" she asked.

"You just dropped my eye into the toilet", I answered. Saying it out loud made things even funnier. I roared! After a few seconds, we started laughing together at the absurdity of the situation. It was one of the first times I could remember laughing since the accident that nearly ended our lives.

Trials are part of life

Resilient people are aware that trials are a common life occurrence. While it may seem that some people have more than their share of tough times, no one is immune to challenges. While I struggle with accepting the tough times with joy, I know that tough times do make us stronger. They also give us a greater depth of empathy and compassion for others. Knowing this encourages us to trust the process and 'plow through it'. As sure as the sun rises in the morning, trials will be a part of all our lives.

> "Count it all joy, my brothers, when you meet trials of various kinds,
> for you know that the testing of your faith produces steadfastness.
> And let steadfastness have its full effect,
> that you may be perfect and complete, lacking in nothing."
> ~ James 1:12

Keep difficult times in perspective

Resilient people know how to react to situations without blowing them out of proportion. They know that over-reacting will cause an absolutely unneeded postponement in surmounting the challenge. Making a mountain out of a molehill requires greater effort and takes more energy and much more time to defeat it.

It is imperative to understand the difference between a

reaction and an over-reaction. There is nothing wrong with a reaction, but it needs to fit the situation. However, when you put more energy into your emotions than the situation requires, it simply wastes your energy and leaves you more frustrated. When you over-react, it exacerbates the situation. It draws attention to your tantrum instead of focusing attention on the problem. It is fine to feel what you feel—and to feel confident enough to say what you feel. It is just as important to know why you are reacting the way that you are.

There are two main types of over-reactors: *internal* and *external*. *Internal* reactors think about an incident over and over again and cannot seem to let it go. *External* over reactors scream, yell, and take out their frustrations on others.

Overreacting makes it impossible to communicate your feelings because you are internalizing them and ruminating about them, or you are externalizing them and distancing yourself from others by your critical words and aggressive actions. Overreacting simply prevents you from solving the problem.

You may have noticed that certain themes creep into your life that cause you to overreact. Any time you overreact to an incident, it is most likely because you are 'triggered'. All of your past negative experiences that remind you of this situation come rushing forward. Therefore, you have a much stronger reaction than you would normally have had if you had simply been dealing with the issue at hand. For example, if you believe that you are never 'heard', you may over-react every time you feel discounted by another person, whether someone cuts in front of you while you are driving or ignores you while you are speaking.

The important thing to remember is that you are justified to feel what you feel, but it is just as important to respond appropriately. Over-reacting simply intensifies the situation. Being cognizant of the difference between reacting and over-reacting will allow you to respond appropriately and it will prevent you from wasting your energy making 'mountains out of molehills'.

An example of this is when I played basketball and

sustained injuries. As a result of spending a lot of time on the court, I was prone to sprained ankles. My doctor explained to me that when ligaments and tendons get stretched in the ankle, it is susceptible to being re-injured. I tried every kind of support and wrap, hoping to heal my ankle quicker—all to no avail.

After experiencing this painful and unrewarding cycle for several years, I was keenly aware that each time I suffered this injury it kept me from playing basketball for at least a month. And each time, I immediately got irritated and depressed. I believed that my life was over for four weeks! I now see that I was making a minor irritation into a major catastrophe. After all, compared to blindness, sprained ankles are a piece of cake.

Try these steps if you have a problem with blowing things out of proportion:

- Identify your triggers
- Look at the situation objectively
- Take several deep breaths to calm down
- Know the difference between responding and reacting
- Do not personalize situations or comments

Live your life by a moral code

Resilient people know the importance of embracing a personal value system. It is critical to have a set of morals and ethics that are above reproach. Regardless of the spiritual belief you subscribe —Buddhist, Christian, Jewish, or New Age, they all call for honesty, integrity and humility. Nearly every religion has its own version of the Golden Rule, which is simply stated as: 'treat others the way you want to be treated.'

Studies indicate that Atheists have a higher suicide rate than those who affiliate with a higher power. Like all statistics, this one is complicated. But I believe that people with strong spiritual beliefs live happier lives than those who don't.

> "This is my commandment, that you love one another
> as I have loved you..."
> ~ John 15:12

"Let each of you look not only to his own interests,
but also to the interests of others."

~ Philippians 2:4

Grow as a result of your challenges
"What does not kill us makes us stronger."

~ Friedrich Nietzsche

I am not a big fan of this Nietzsche quote. It seems rather fatalistic and implies that if you live, you will become stronger. That is not the case. Instead, I prefer this from Chuck Swindoll:

"The longer I live, the more convinced I become that life is 10 percent what happens to us and 90 percent how we respond to it."

This short homily recognizes that being resilient and overcoming your challenges is a choice that is entirely up to you.

Bethany Hamilton is a great example of 'bouncing back'. At the young age of thirteen, while surfing in Hawaii, a fourteen-foot tiger shark attacked Bethany, severing her arm. After she recovered, she continued to enter surfing competitions. She eventually won a national surfing championship. She followed up by writing and publishing her autobiography called, *Soul Surfer: A true story of faith, family and fighting to get back on the board*. Shortly thereafter, this inspirational book was made into a movie. As of this writing, Bethany is twenty-five years old, happily married, and the mother of a little boy. And... she is still surfing! What an amazing example of growth in spite of facing what seemed to be insurmountable obstacles.

Recognize your strengths and weaknesses

Resilient people are self-actualized. They know who they are—and who they are not. They know they are not perfect, but they are fully aware of their positive strengths.

First, make a list of your strengths and weaknesses. No one else will see this list, so be totally candid. Your list may include personal characteristics, traits, and attitudes. This is all about being, not about doing. Therefore, accomplish-ments do not belong on this list. Examples of your positive characteristics might include: I am intelligent. I am generous. I am confident—and so forth. If you are feeling brave, you may ask those around you for their input. Once you complete your list of strengths, look it over. Give yourself the accolades that you deserve.

Then, analyze your weaknesses. This is a thoughtful list of the characteristics that you want to develop or improve upon, like: I am judgmental. I am dishonest. I am stingy.

Now come up with a plan. Prioritize each item that you have listed. Which ones do you want to work on first? Figure out how you can turn your weaknesses into strengths.

Lacking an empathy chip? Help out at a local Hospice center. Having problems with honesty? Get an accountability partner. Feeling selfish? Volunteer at a social service agency.

Do not judge others

Resilient people understand that they must get to know a person before passing judgment. Resilient people are aware that focusing on the behaviors of others is a waste of time and energy. By keeping negative judgments at bay, a truly resilient person can steer lots of added energy in more productive, positive directions.

In his famous 'I have a dream' speech, Martin Luther King, Jr. said: "I have a dream that my four little children will one day live in a nation where they will not be judged by the color of their skin but by the content of their character."

This dream not only applies to racial strife, but also to just about any other group of people who are different. Many people judge others by their politics (conservative or liberal), religion (Christian or Muslim), socio-economic status (rich or poor), gender (male or female), education (college graduate or high school dropout), or even geographic location (east or west; north or south). Judgments of differences become so ridiculous that people judge others by whether they are dog or cat lovers.

If you put people in a box before you get a chance to know them, you will fail to see their true character. The next time you run into someone on the other side of the fence, make a dedicated effort to get to know the person before you make an assumption about who they are. You might be surprised. For instance, I discovered that people who are cat lovers are not as crazy as I had thought them to be!

If you find that you struggle to keep a positive attitude, the first step is to recognize the source of it and own it. So many people have bad attitudes and don't even know it! Or, they know that they have a bad attitude but try to deny it. Neither approach works. There are some relatively easy steps you can take to improve your attitude.

Step 1. Use the power of positive thinking

The Saturday Night Live skit with Stuart Smalley may sound ridiculous: *"I'm good enough, I'm smart enough, and, doggone it, people like me,"* he intones. But, truth be told, studies prove that positive self-talk really works.

Positive thinking begins with positive self-talk. Self-talk is when you provide opinions and evaluations on what you are doing as you are doing it. If you are a negative person, this self-talk is destructive. Psychologists often call negative self-talk 'parent tapes'. It doesn't necessarily mean that your parents were negative; it means the voice in your head is constantly berating you. ("I'm worthless", "I'm stupid", and "I will never be happy"). These thoughts are based on incorrect assumptions or they transpire from a negative attitude. Here are some suggestions for developing **positive self-talk:**

- Intentionally tell yourself your positive characteristics. Talk to yourself the way you would talk to a friend. Most likely, you wouldn't say something negative to someone else, therefore, don't say it to yourself;
- Do 'check-ups' on your mental attitude throughout the day. If your brain is saying negative things, say 'stop'! This is distorted thinking. Then immediately replace the negative thought with a positive thought.
- Identify areas that need improvement. Are there areas in your life in which you are more negative than you are in other areas? Do you criticize

yourself regarding how you do a task? Whether you are at the weight you want to be? Whether you exercise enough? Whether you complete projects? Whether you communicate effectively with your family? If so, start your positive self-talk program there.

In addition to improving your outlook on life, another great reason to be a positive thinker is for the health benefits. Positive people have:

- Lower risks of cardiovascular disease
- Longer life expectancies
- Better immune systems
- Overall improvement in physical and mental health

Step 2. Read a self-help or inspirational book

Reading a self-help book or an inspirational story about someone who has overcome challenges can help you re-evaluate your own life. By reading about the skills and techniques others have embraced in order to triumph over adversity, you can employ these same skills in your own life.

I have been awed and humbled by people who have told me that my book, *The World at My Fingertips,* has helped them to work through their own personal challenges. It was never my goal to be an inspirational author. To be quite honest, before the accident, I had never read a book of this genre. I often say, "I am just an average guy who went through a horrific accident." With God's help, and that of my family and friends, I was able to come out the other of a tragedy intact and thriving. How could I not tell my story?

In the ever-expanding universe of e-books and self-publishing, there are thousands of books like mine that are available. Search Amazon and choose a book that 'speaks' to you.

Step 3. Seek professional help

An objective professional can give you the tools that you need to improve your negative attitude. You have qualified people to choose from: a cognitive behavioral counselor, a life coach, a pastor, or a rabbi. These people, who have expertise in helping you improve your attitude, increase your self-esteem, encourage you to create a gratitude list and give you the tools you will need to help you deal with your issues in an effective way.

Prior generations believed that the only people who sought help from a therapist were people who were mentally ill. Today, most people understand that nearly everyone would benefit by seeking counsel from a therapist. A qualified therapist will be objective and will help you to see your situation from a different perspective. A therapist will help you to focus on the things that you can change—and encourage you to let go of the things you cannot. Therapists are trained to help you look at the past without regretting it and to enjoy the moment without fearing the future.

Step 4. See a Psychiatrist or Family Physician

Your issues may be the result of a chemical imbalance. In spite of the fact that the brain is the most complex organ of the body, people tend to discount medications that would help their brain to work at its optimal level. When a chemical imbalance transpires, it can trigger depression, irritability, anxiety or other behavioral issues. If your brain is lacking (or producing too much) serotonin, norepinephrine or dopamine, no amount of positive thinking, reading self-help books, or even attending counseling sessions, will optimally work until you seek the help of a psychiatrist or a family doctor. A medical professional can determine whether medication is needed. Then, when you believe that you can think clearly, that your brain is once again working on all its cylinders, see a licensed therapist or psychologist to talk through the issues that bother you. Studies show that talking about a troubling issue reduces the power that it has over you. The problem then dissipates.

Maintaining a positive attitude is the key to living a productive, happy life. It will set the foundation for the things that you want to accomplish.

> "Keep your face always toward the sunshine–
> and shadows will fall behind you."
>
> ~ Walt Whitman

Chapter 5
The Resiliency Triangle: Commitment to Goals

> "But as for you, be strong and do not give up,
> for your work will be rewarded."
> ~ 2 Chronicles 15:7

Resilient people are committed to accomplishing their life goals. They know it is important to set and then achieve their objectives in order to fulfill their purpose. It is evident that successful people such as CEOs, professional athletes, and top entertainers did not achieve their goals by accident. They succeeded by setting up—then working— a plan.

Successful people are great at setting both short-term and long-term goals. Short-term goals establish the blueprint for victory. In order to reach long-term goals, you must be motivated, persistent and self-disciplined.

The process is very much like sailing a boat to a specific destination. For example, if you wanted to sail from San Diego to Hawaii, you wouldn't just show up at the marina, jump on a sailboat, and head out to sea. No, you would plan the course to your destination with meticulous attention to detail. You would secure a sturdy craft for the long voyage, stock your provisions: including a map, compass and GPS system to keep you on course. To accomplish your life goals, you need the same type of plan.

Where to start

First, you need to establish goals for all the vital aspects of your life. This comprehensive approach will help keep you well balanced and provide you with a variety of growth experiences. If you set goals in only one area of your life, you will live and die in that one area—and only muddle along, severely out of balance in all the others. Your life will be much more invigorating if you set goals in every area of your life.

Suggested goal-setting categories

- Family – Do you want to get married? Start a family?
- Education – What level of education do you want to acquire?
- Career – What do you want to accomplish before you retire?
- Financial – How much money do you want to make? Save? Give away?
- Personality – Is there an aspect of your personality you want to change?
- Hobbies – Is there something you want to learn, like photography, woodworking, playing an instrument?
- Physical – Do you want to make any body changes, like lose weight, get in better shape, run a marathon, learn to snow ski?
- Travel – Is there somewhere you want to visit... Europe, Australia, or the Swiss Alps?
- Volunteer – Do you want to give back by volunteering your time to a social service agency?
- Spiritual – Do you want to strengthen your relation-ship with God?

After setting your overall life goals, back off and take the 35,000-foot view of what you want your life to look like—in the long term—in each of the above categories. Distancing yourself from the details and looking at the big picture will help you focus on the energy you must expend.

And, by the way, only you can determine the length of time for your long-term goals. It could be two years, five years, ten years, or even twenty years, depending on your age and your current station in life.

Invest significant time on this project. Don't try to do it all in one sitting. Take an hour's 'think-break' every day, over several days, to be sure you are enthusiastic about the goals you have set.

Try to 'play the movie forward'. Imagine yourself at age 75 looking back on your life. Are there goals that you failed to achieve? Do you feel disappointed? If so, write down the items that you wish to fulfill.

If you have too many goals, narrow them down. The objective here is to develop one or two goals in each life category without overlooking anything. From there, you may want to narrow your plan to just the goals in which you are most passionate. Make sure they are achievements or realizations that are important to *you*—not to your parents, your family, or your employer.

Finally, plot your path toward each goal by breaking it down into individual steps that you can easily implement on a daily, weekly and monthly basis. Your initial attempt of planning each goal may involve more research than action.

As you contemplate each goal, you may find yourself modifying it—or even deleting the item entirely. It's better to discover potential problems when you are early in the process, rather than spending years trying to achieve the impossible. What if you spent much time and energy only to find out that a given achievement wasn't as important as you once thought? It's much better to evaluate potentially negative outcomes in advance.

Just as you would need to refer to your map if you were sailing from San Diego to Hawaii, your life course will need occasional corrections. That is to say that it's wise to examine each goal as you move toward it, taking corrective actions where and when needed. Believe me, this happens often in life because no one can accurately predict the future. So put a note on your calendar to check your progress and perform any corrections on a scheduled basis. Continually updating your course will keep you on target for a successful journey.

> "I have begun everything with the idea that I could succeed, and I never had much patience with the multitudes of people who are always ready to explain why one cannot succeed."
>
> ~ Booker T. Washington

Let me show you how I used this model to achieve some important goals in my life after I became blind. Here is the big picture:

- Career – To own and operate my own insurance agency
- Physical – To learn to snow ski again
- Hobby – To learn to play the guitar again
- Volunteer – To give time, energy and money to the Arizona Center for the Blind and Visually Impaired

Using the career goal, here is how I broke it down into smaller steps:

- *Five-year goal* – To own and operate my own insurance agency
- *One-year goal* – To locate and be in negotiations to purchase an existing agency
- *One-month goal* – To contact colleagues in the insurance industry and business brokers to search for agencies that were for sale.
- *One-week goal* – To complete a pro forma business plan to determine if agency ownership was viable. To contact insurance associations to see if there were other blind insurance agents.

My plan became a great example of goals that needed to be modified. My one week, one month, and one year goals all went swimmingly. I discovered that there were indeed many blind insurance agents. I ran the numbers and found that I could expect to be running a profitable agency within two years. By contacting colleagues in the business, I found an agent who wanted to sell his agency because he was retiring. We negotiated the purchase agreement. Then the wheels came off.

At the last minute, the seller decided that he didn't want to retire. Unfortunately, in great anticipation of my new agency, I had already leased an office space, hired an assistant, and lined up my company appointments. It was time to go back to the drawing board.

Going back to my one-week goal, I projected the numbers for a start-up agency. While I did not have an immediate income stream, I also did not have a debt service for the purchase. I estimated it would take me three years to break even. I pushed forward with my revised plan and was able to successfully accomplish my five-year goal. It required a major course correction at the last minute, but I did it!

"Success always leaves footprints."
~ Booker T. Washington

Studies show that if you document your goals, rather than just think about them, you are twice as likely to achieve them. That is an impressive improvement in your success rate that expends very little effort.

ε

One goal-setting strategy I have found to be very effective is the **_SMART_** mnemonic:

S -Specific or Significant

Set a specific, significant goal. Then establish a well thought out plan with succinct actions in order to achieve that goal. Vague goals are destined for the rust heap.

M -Measurable or Meaningful

Include a way to track your progress. When goals are measurable, you are far more likely to achieve them. Many smart-phone apps are available to help you measure your progress. Or, go 'old school' and just write your goals down on paper.

A -Attainable or Action oriented

Set realistic goals. Most people find it difficult to stay motivated when they set their goals too high or too low. Make sure your goals are realistically achievable. If not, lower the bar a bit.

R -Relevant or Rewarding

Set goals that are pertinent to you. These goals should be ones that you believe in and are willing to work toward. When you choose goals that align with your personal value system and ones that you are passionate about, you will be motivated to achieve them.

T = Time bound or Trackable

Make sure your goal is anchored with a time frame or is otherwise trackable. This step should specifically state what you plan to accomplish and when you plan to achieve it. And remember, the timeline for most goals needs to be modified from time to time.

ଧ

Let me give you a personal example of how I employed the **_SMART_** method. As difficult as it may be to believe, before my accident I didn't know how to type. The old 'hunt and peck' method got me through college and worked just fine in my professional career. (My emails were very short.) Although, after the accident, I quickly realized that the only way I was going to be able to communicate with the outside world, via the written word, was to learn to type. The screen reading program for the blind that I wanted to master, was 100% reliant on the keyboard. No more dodging it, I had to acquire the skills to find my way around the keyboard.

Here is how I applied **_SMART_**.

Specific

Easy! I needed to learn to become proficient by using a keyboard with my eyes closed (so to speak). What was my plan of action to accomplish this? My extremely loving and patient wife, Kristi, who volunteered to teach me.

Measurable

I decided to learn one row of letters each week by spending at least thirty minutes practicing each day, five days a week.

Achievable

After I came home from the hospital and while recuperating from the accident, I had plenty of time to devote to this task. I also knew blind people who were very proficient typists. The fact that typing students were required to type without looking at the keyboard told me something: *it could be done!*

Relevant

It was clear to me that learning to type was going to improve my life in many ways. It would allow me to communicate by sending and receiving emails, to type documents, and to surf the web. Perhaps most importantly, it would give me the skills I needed to get back into the workforce.

My timeline...

I wanted to become a proficient typist in two months. I believed it would take one week to learn each of the three rows of letters, another week to learn the other keys, and a month of practice, practice, practice.

...and the result?

Well, obviously, I accomplished this goal. I learned to type in two months. I typed the lyrics to Gilligan's Island theme song so many times I began to feel like I was marooned on a deserted island (and, in many ways, I was). With this newly found skill, I was able to return to work, keep my personal records (calendar, phone numbers, addresses, etc.), communicate via email, surf the web with the best of them—and write a book. I do not know how many words I can type per minute, but let's just say, I am fast!

> "Ninety-nine percent of the failures come
> from people who have the habit
> of making excuses."
> ~ George Washington Carver

Earlier, I mentioned that you would increase the odds of accomplishing your goals by documenting them. A recent survey presented the following probability to successfully achieve a goal. Take a good look at these:

Thinking about a goal – 10% probability of success

Consciously deciding to set a goal – 25% probability of success

Assigning a timetable to the goal – 40% probability of success

Designing a plan to act on the goal – 50% probability of success

Telling another about your goal – 65% probability of success

Being accountable to another person – 95% probability of success

These numbers demonstrate that if you are serious about accomplishing your goals, you must put in the effort. When you have an accountability partner, your success rate is substantially increased. Your partner in this exercise should be someone with whom you share your entire plan. You should also set up specific times when you will meet with your partner to discuss obstacles that you are facing, possible corrections to make, and milestones you have hit.

Examples of successful groups who teach accountability are the twelve-step programs such as AA (Alcoholics Anonymous), NA (Narcotics Anonymous), GA (Gamblers Anonymous), OA (Overeaters Anonymous), and ALANON.

Those individuals who overcome their challenges and reach great heights know that as long as they talk about their fears, recognize what makes them stumble, and keep their eye on the prize, they will succeed.

As you set new goals, it is also imperative to understand that it will take time for those lifestyle changes to become habits. You need to be patient and look toward the long-term benefits rather than to expect the 'quick fix'.

You may have heard the concept that it takes 21 days to establish a new habit. Unfortunately, new research reveals that this is untrue. The 21-day myth was proposed in the early 1960s and was not based on scientific research. It sounded good. Several famous self-help gurus quoted this theory. Unfortunately, it was inaccurate.

A current study indicates that there is no magic number in establishing a new habit. It depends on many factors, including the habit, the person and many other external factors. That said, studies have demonstrated that it can take anywhere from two months to eight months to establish a new habit. But, don't despair. Look at the positives:

- In the big picture, two to eight months is not very long to build a healthy behavior.
- You do not have to do (or not do) something every day to be effective. It is OK if you miss a day or two every now and then.
- Quick fixes usually don't work. By allowing more time for habits to become automatic, you can implement them with smaller steps and make changes as you go.

Regardless of whether it takes 21 days or eight months, you need to start with day one. You need to be dedicated to the goal of implementing the habit, and then do the work to make it a part of your life.

A quick word about time management. I believe that one of the major stumbling blocks that prevent people from accomplishing their goals or implementing good habits is that they have poor time management. It has always amazed me how much time people can waste doing irrelevant or unimportant tasks. It is OK to take a walk in the 'tall weeds' from time to time, but one must not spend the majority of the day there.

When I managed a team at a commercial insurance company, I was very frustrated at the amount of time people wasted by talking about anything other than work- sports, movies, restaurants, kids, you name it. Don't get me wrong, a few minutes chatting about these things is fine, but these people could spend the majority of the day discussing the best place to get a pizza. I think some of these folks were lucky to get twenty minutes of work in every hour. It drove me nuts.

One day, after one of my team members had spent thirty minutes on a fifteen-minute break, discussing the pros and cons of a designated hitter, I knew something needed to be done. The next day, after he left for one of his extended breaks, I had the entire team sign a 'Thanks for coming back to work!' card and left it on his desk. That was the last time we had that problem.

I also had a team-member who was abysmal at time management and prioritizing tasks. She was a great person, professionally and personally, but her lack of time management skills really hurt her performance. To solve the problem, I scheduled a time management course. On the day of the class, she failed to show up. When I walked to her desk, I found her there frantically working. I asked why she was not in the class and she responded that she had too much work to do and didn't have time to attend the class. And besides, she said, "I have taken those classes before and I know all about time management."

I believe that a lot of people with time management and prioritization issues are unaware that they have them. Conversely, there are others who are hyperaware of the time they waste. Regardless of which category you fall into, it would benefit you to look into improving your time management skills. There are so many great time management programs to choose from, that it would be counter-productive to list them here. I suggest you Google 'time management tips' or search the app store on your smart phone. Find a plan that works for you. Whether you are a type A or a type B person, you will have several plans to choose from that fit your personality.

Remember—one of the keys to good time management is the ability to prioritize the tasks and stick with the plan. Nothing can throw a monkey wrench into a good time management plan faster than spending extended periods of time on low-level tasks while ignoring priority items. Sometimes, the priority items are not all that time consuming.

They are just tasks that you don't want to tackle for one reason or another. Often times, once completed, you discover the task was not as troublesome as you initially thought.

Personally, I have always been pretty good at prioritizing. Not to say that I can't waste time with the best of them, surfing the net or listening to a ball game, but I usually have the ability to get back on track quickly. I recognize that not everyone has this attribute.

You may have noticed that I have not mentioned the dreaded 'P' word—*Procrastination*. Nothing can kill a goal faster than procrastinating. You can't win the race if your horse never leaves the starting gate. You can have the best set of goals in the world, the most effective goal-setting model, the most efficient time management plan. But, if you are a procrastinator, those well-meaning goals will never see the light of day. Perhaps you need to make correcting your procrastination problem the first item on your goal list.

So, what are you waiting for? Quit procrastinating! Put your goals in place. Develop a plan to accomplish those goals, assign an accountability partner and learn how to effectively manage your time. Before you know it, you will be crossing the gangplank for your well-planned sail to Hawaii!

Twenty years from now you will be more disappointed by the things
that you didn't do than by the ones you did do.
So throw off the bowlines. Sail away from the safe harbor.
Catch the trade winds in your sails. Explore. Dream. Discover.
~H. Jackson Brown, Jr.

Chapter 6
The Resiliency Triangle:
A Strong Support System

"Two are better than one, because they have a good return
for their work: If one falls down, his friend can help him up.
But pity the man who falls and has no oneto help him up."

~ Ecclesiastes 4:9

Resilient people have a strong support system. The medical
definition of a support system is 'a network of people who
provide an individual with practical or emotional support'. You
know, the people who stand on the sidelines—cheering for you,
encouraging you to keep pushing forward until you reach your
goals. A support system is to provide you with positive
reassurance that your goals are realistic, achievable and
worthwhile. In order to be resilient, you must have a strong
support team. This team is an integral component of the
Resiliency Triangle.

You may be pleasantly surprised by who ends up supporting
and unfortunately, disappointed by those who do not.
Interestingly enough, oftentimes the people you think will be
there for you in a time of crisis, simply cannot (or will not) step
up to the plate. In a perfect world, you would hope that your
spouse, partner, family, and close friends would be there for you.
But, if they are not understanding and supportive, you may need
to distance yourself (emotionally) from these people and look
elsewhere for strength.

Sometimes, people you know only by acquaintance may
step up to help you. Perhaps these individuals may have
suffered loss or trauma and can be a tower of strength for you.

Or it may be people who simply believe in your cause and/or your purpose. Supportive people understand that they cannot tell you that they know how you feel or compare your losses to theirs. They will just listen with compassion and know that you need to talk about your loss without fear of judgment.

> "Listen to advice and accept instruction,
> that you may gain wisdom in the future."
> ~ Proverbs 19:20

*There are many places where you may find
a strong support team*

Faith-based support

If you practice a religion, check in with your local church, synagogue, or similar organization to discover if they offer support groups. Our church offers support groups for just about any topic that you can imagine, including divorce, depression, grief, loss, and addictions.

Professional support

You may find it very effective to enlist the help of a professional. This could be a counselor, life-coach, or a psychologist. These people can teach you the tools you'll need to accomplish your goals. If you elect to go this route, be sure to select professionals who specialize in your particular area. For example, if you are seeking grief counseling, you need to look for a counselor who is specifically trained in grief and loss. It only makes sense that you will get better (and more objective) tools from a licensed counselor than you would from a friend or a family member.

Addiction rehabilitation

It goes without saying that if a person is in the throes of an addiction, rehabilitation is required before resiliency skills can be effectively acquired. Professionals now under-stand that addiction is the consequence of an addictive brain. Some people's brains are wired to be more at risk for addiction. These addictions can include alcohol, drugs, sex, tobacco, shopping, gambling, and eating. While there is much debate about whether the phenomenon of addiction is physical and/or mental, there is no doubt the addiction exists. The bottom line is that addictions ruin lives. An addiction can happen to anyone, at any socio-economic level, at any age, regardless of gender. Decades of studies demonstrate that the most effective method of rehabilitating addicts is through a residential inpatient facility. Addiction counselors are equipped with the skills and expertise to assist individuals through these life-threatening challenges.

A word of warning: if you or a loved one is in need of help, understand that rehabilitation has become a big business in the United States. Do your homework before committing to a particular center. Check online reviews (not the reviews written on the facility's website). Visit the facility. Interview the staff. Educate yourself regarding the different counseling theories. The time you invest in this investigation will pay off. Rehab is extremely expensive. Make sure you are getting the best program available for you or your loved one.

Addiction rehabilitation is an extremely complicated and emotional issue. Overcoming an addiction requires a complete lifestyle change. It is not my intention to drill down any further. I only want to reiterate the point that one must seek a specialized, dedicated support group to successfully battle this growing epidemic that plagues our society.

> "No temptation has overtaken you
> that is not common to man.
> God is faithful, and he will not let you
> be tempted beyond your ability,
> but with the temptation he will also provide
> the way of escape,
> that you may be able to endure it."
> ~ 1 Corinthians 10:13

Support groups

Think of any problem that you can imagine and you will find a support group for it. Support groups are popular because they are effective. Sharing your hopes and dreams, challenges and tribulations with people who are also facing the same issues can give you unique insight. Sharing your issues with others also provides you with accountability partners.

Volunteer opportunities

This may seem like an unusual place to find a support group, but studies show that one of the greatest ways to overcome loss or depression is to volunteer. You will find that volunteering encourages you to focus on others instead of yourself. Volunteering your time to help others builds your confidence and provides you with a sense of purpose. You may also find that you have a 'ready-made' support team consisting of the volunteers that you meet.

To find a place to volunteer, research non-profit organizations that touch your heart. Check their websites for volunteer opportunities. If you can't think of any specific group, just Google some areas of personal interest and investigate the opportunities. Make it a homework assignment. Create a 'top five' list, and then call the organization. My guess is that one or two of them will peak your interest. Then, before you know it, you will be helping others, and in turn, they will be helping you.

Now let's look at some helpful tips
for building a strong support system

Look over your professional and personal life. Identify occasions or periods of time in which you were successful. Recall which tools you utilized at that time. Take a look at the support team that helped you along the way. Where did these people come from? Are they avenues you could once again draw upon to help you today? Here are the steps to take:

- Develop a list of the areas in your life that you could use a strong support group. Be sure to include your business and personal life. Select some emotionally healthy people whom you trust and believe in, to help you come up with your blueprint for success.

- Meet individually with each person and solicit him or her for advice on how you can build your support team. Come up with a list of specific questions, such as: Who is on your support team? How did you find them? Is there a helpful program/club/group/website that you would suggest? Do you have any tips that you can give me to help my situation?
- Assign an accountability partner. Find at least one emotionally healthy person in whom you trust. Find one who is willing to help you achieve your goals. Sit down with him/her and share your plan. Ask for suggestions and improvements in your plan. Come up with a timeline for regular 'check in' sessions. Be prepared to modify your plan or change the timeline if needed.

After the auto accident which left me blind, I was both encouraged and saddened by people's reactions. Fortunately, the true supporters greatly outnumbered those who were unable to be supportive of me. I give a great deal of credit to my family and friends who helped through those dark days.

First and foremost was my wife, Kristi. It was clear to me, right from those early days in the hospital, that she was going to be there for me. Kristi recognized that she was there to support me in a much different fashion than she had before the accident. I was dealing with a major brain injury that caused cognitive issues in even the simplest of tasks. Many wives would have packed their bags and moved on. As a matter of fact, studies show that 85 to 90 percent of all marriages fail after a significant crisis. But Kristi rolled up her sleeves and got to work, finding me the best medical care available. I always looked forward to her visiting me in the hospital and felt a great sense of relief that she would continue to be with me on my painful journey.

After returning home, I remained in a fragile mental state for several months. Kristi continued to encourage me, helping me to deal with my day-to-day life as a blind person. Compounding her challenges, understandably, were her broken collarbones, fractured foot and her own head injury. With all the attention focused on me, her traumatic brain injury went unrecognized by almost everyone. Honestly, at times, her memory and cognitive problems were worse than mine. It was a very difficult time, but we got through it—together.

Over the years, Kristi has continued to be the lead person on my support team. Regardless of what I have gone through (ongoing surgeries, fatherhood, going back to work, writing a book, or motivational speaking) she has unequivocally been my harbor in the storm and my biggest cheerleader.

My family has offered much support over the years since the accident, in different ways and at different times. Some stepped up in the early days, like my mom, who wouldn't leave my bedside, and my sister Janice, who was, thankfully, on a sabbatical at the time and offered a listening ear and drove both Kristi and me to our many doctor appointments. Others provided me with the care and support I needed later on. Some became more involved after I got home and was struggling to re-integrate into 'regular' life. My dad was instrumental in helping me get my insurance agency up and running. My brother Jim and sister Cheryl assisted me in operating the agency, while other family members, including my niece, Tawnya, were always available to take me to my speaking engagements. Regardless of how and when they helped, they have each been preciously valuable to me. With them, I have been able to build a new life. I realize this is not a given.

Several of my pre-accident friends have been supportive during my long journey to overcome my blindness. They have helped me reintegrate socially, which has been extremely important to me. Thanks to my friends, I have been able to go snow skiing, attend sporting events, join bible studies and go out to dinner with the guys. When I'm with my friends, they treat me like they did before—like I am just one of the guys.

Well, maybe they do cut me a little slack, but, at the same time, they keep me on my toes.

Golf is a pastime in which I found an unlikely support system. A couple of months after the accident, some of my family members, close friends and even business colleagues, hosted a golf tournament to help Kristi and me defer some of our staggering medical costs. The money was helpful, but the outpouring of love and support was priceless. I will never forget that so many people cared enough about us to host this generous event. Welker Charities went on to hold ten annual golf tournaments, donating over $200,000 to the Arizona Center for the Blind and Visually Impaired. Every year, I met more people who ultimately expanded my universe of recovery by becoming active members of my support team.

If you know someone who is struggling, why don't you choose to be on his or her support team? Consider organizing a fundraiser to help out—financially and/or emotionally. It doesn't have to be a golf tournament. It could be a bowl-a-thon, bike ride, walk-a-thon, marathon, or a go fund me account. Use your imagination. Find out what hobbies interest your friend. Google 'fundraising activities'. There are some great ideas online.

Getting to golf with my buddies is a more casual affair these days, but I do not, for a moment, take for granted how important their support is to me. They drive me to the course, guide me to the cart, drive me from hole to hole, set up my shots, and try to find the balls I have hit into the desert. No easy task! Without my golf support team, I would not be able to participate in this wonderfully rewarding (and sometimes extremely frustrating) activity. My advice is to take up a sport or group activity that you can share with others. These activities will help you to build your support team.

Unexpected additions to my personal support team were 'new' friends (post-accident friends). While many disabled people have a tough time making friends, I have been extremely blessed. God has placed many new friends in my life. People came out of the woodwork to provide us with every kind of help. Before I got home from the hospital, a Sunday school class at our church volunteered to bring us dinners. We had a different meal every night for three months. Kristi could not drive because of her extensive injuries; so, new friends provided her rides to the hospital so she could visit me. The list goes on and on to include dozens of people who stepped forward to help us, including some we didn't even know.

Leeza Gibbons was a prominent member of our support team. Kristi and I had videotaped an episode of her show just two weeks before our accident. We talked about the impending birth of our miracle babies. (Ironically, this show aired two days after our accident.) When Leeza heard about the tragedy, she supported us by sending cards and gifts and regularly checking in on us. She invited us back to her show several times after the accident to update her audience about our progress.

Leeza's personal interest in us helped immensely in our healing process. It helped us to accept that people, besides the two of us, believed our tragedy was a big deal. This assisted me in understanding the magnitude of the tragedy, while at the same time it encouraged me to embrace the tools that were required to overcome my loss and to thrive in spite of it.

I realize that not everyone is going to have a celebrity on his or her support team. It was a matter of the stars aligning (and, quite simply, pure luck) that Leeza came into our lives when she did. The point is this: don't set your sights too low when looking for a supporter. That supporter could come from anywhere. Just keep your eyes open and aim high.

Business colleagues were another very important addition to my support team, one I initially underestimated. They 'circled the wagons' around me and provided support in a myriad of ways. In the early days, they helped with meals, provided transportation, and watched our babies. They provided social encouragement by taking me to sporting events, concerts, shopping—or just simply to lunch. It is important to note that not all of these work colleagues were people with whom I had been close. Some were people I barely knew. But they were folks who knew how to support someone in need. When you look for people to be on your support team, don't forget to look at those you work with. They may surprise you.

A very important, and unexpected, part of my support team came from the volunteer work I provided for two organizations: The Arizona Center for the Blind and Visually Impaired (ACBVI) and The Valley of the Sun United Way. Volunteering for these organizations helped me to develop a sense of self-worth and to find a purpose in my life. I made a lot of friends, and I became aware of the fact that there were more people fighting disabilities than I could have ever imagined. Working for an agency that helped people like me (ACBVI) made me feel as though I had a semblance of control over my own disability. Before our accident, I had no idea that so many philanthropic organizations existed. When I spoke for the United Way, the employees made me feel like a celebrity. This did wonders for my bruised ego. Over the years, I've done hundreds of presentations for them.

These days, I have added a couple of new organizations to my 'volunteer' support team: The Lions Club and Guide Dogs of the Desert. These are two organizations I believe in and they believe in me. I speak frequently on behalf of these two causes and they have given me great purpose in my life.

One of the Lions' primary objectives is to support the blind and visually impaired. My club, the Chandler Lions, financially supports ACBVI and Guide Dogs of the Desert. So you can see that while I am helping them, they are helping organizations near and dear to my heart. I have made many new friends through the Lions and the Guide Dogs of the Desert, which allows me to add more active and empathetic members to my support team—both two and four-legged. These are special causes, and the people affiliated with them are extraordinary. I feel privileged that these outstanding organizations have asked me to be one of their ambassadors.

Be sure to check out civic groups, social service organizations, church groups, and other similar volunteer opportunities, when you search for more individuals to join your support group.

Regardless of where they came from, I understand that I am very blessed to have such a strong team. Although, be aware that you don't need to have a plethora of them. Your team may consist of only one or two people. The only criteria are that they are emotionally healthy, having your best interests at heart and truly wanting you to overcome your challenges.

Do not be deceived:
"Bad company corrupts good morals."
~ 1 Corinthians 15:33

It is just as important to be aware of who should not be part of your support team. Just because someone is a close friend, family member, or even your spouse, that does not necessarily mean they are qualified to be on your support team. Some people have issues of their own and simply cannot be available for you. Perhaps they are co-dependent and feel a need to 'help' you, even if 'help' is not in your best interest. Unfortunately, some people may have their own agenda and may want you to be dependent upon them.

After the accident, I was extremely disappointed by some of the people who I thought were my friends. A few seemed unable to accept me as a blind person and they just dropped out of my life. As time went by, I realized that the distance they created between us, was really their problem, not mine. Their lack of empathy and their inability to be comfortable around me was their issue. I couldn't let it be mine. I had to accept that these people were simply incapable of providing support for me or, for that matter, perhaps anyone else.

If you are going through difficult times and have noticed a similar phenomenon regarding people you had thought would be in your corner; don't waste your time and energy trying to figure out why they aren't. There is probably nothing that you can do to change their way of thinking or acting. Instead, focus your energy and effort (and gratitude) on the people who have shown a real, heartfelt interest in helping you move forward with your life. You need positive people, not negative ones, around you. Unhealthy, toxic people will only drag you down.

I like the 'crab-in-a-bucket' analogy. If you put a lone crab in a bucket, it will eventually use its claws and climb out. But if you put two crabs in the same bucket, as the first crab is trying to pull itself out, the second one will pull it down to the bottom once again.

> "There are two ways of exerting one's strength;
> one is pushing down, the other is pulling up."
> ~ Booker T. Washington

Kristi and I believe that one of the most difficult times you will have, when you are struggling with a trauma or loss, will be to find a safe person in whom you can confide your fears and share your hope. The two of us were fortunate to have several people who rallied around us without reservation. Unfortunately, after the car accident, we each discovered several people who could not accept the emotional and physical changes that we had made. Research shows that many people change emotionally after a crisis. They look at life differently. Energy that they may have expended in the past, on minor issues, no longer seem important. Unless a potential supporter truly understands trauma and/or depression, or is patient enough to learn what you need, they cannot (or will not) understand what you are and are not capable of.

Here is how I see it: Each one of us has one cylinder of energy a day, and when all that available energy is used just trying to 'bounce back' and 'overcome', you do not have energy for much else. Both Kristi and I are completely familiar with the destructive power of a physical disability. Our best supporters are those who, in spite of not having experienced it, can empathize and continue to contribute whatever and whenever they can.

Often, when times get tough, family and friends disappear. In fact, many families totally disintegrate when there is a crisis. Individuals who have not suffered a 'life altering' event have great difficulty understanding why you are different and why you no longer have the energy to 'sweat the small stuff'. Some people had the audacity to tell Kristi that they wanted the 'old'

Kristi back. Of course, that is asking for the impossible. No one can go through what we went through without undergoing massive emotional changes. Fortunately, many of these changes are positive ones. Research illustrates that many people who endure grave challenges or crises, have a greater depth of empathy and compassion for others. Many acquire better boundaries, no longer taking on more than they can handle.

During these times of stress, be cognizant that much of your energy needs to go toward dealing with the current crisis. Which means that people who drain what little energy you have, need to be loved from a distance. Surround yourself with emotionally healthy people.

Many times it is difficult to determine who is emotionally healthy and who is not. Much has been written on this topic, including Dr. Henry Cloud, who wrote a book entitled *Safe People*. Here are some characteristics that he says define unsafe people:

- People who lack friends. There is usually a reason for this.
- People who avoid being vulnerable. They are avoiding intimacy, communicating only on a superficial level. They withhold parts of themselves hoping that you will believe they have it 'all together.'
- People who cannot tolerate criticism even when it's constructive. Unable to admit fault, these people justify their actions and focus on your faults. When you try to tell them that you are hurt by their behavior, they make it about themselves, refusing to see the situation from your perspective.
- People who lie to you instead of telling you the truth; in spite of this, they demand your trust.
- People who gossip about you, instead of keeping your secrets confidential. They run from one person to another "stirring the pot".
- People who are inconsistent. They don't live up to their commitments. They make promises they

cannot keep. They lack integrity. They are out to get their needs met, without considering the needs of others.

- People who give you advice when you don't ask for it. They don't trust your judgment. Critical and disapproving, they are quite certain that, without them, you will not make the right decisions.
- They are enmeshed. This occurs when the person wants nearly all your time, and is competitive and jealous when you have other friends or other interests.

So how do you create an emotionally healthy relationship? What do safe people look like? They are honest, supportive, loyal (they have your back), trusting, able to give as well as receive (although they don't keep score), and they encourage you to have a rich, full life (instead of holding on and smothering you).

Healthy people respect your ideas. They recognize that their way is not always the right way. They stand up for you when you have been wronged. They respect you as an individual, and celebrate your differences. They accept you for all facets of your personality; the good, the bad and the ugly. Quite simply, an emotionally healthy person will always encourage you to be the best person you can be.

"Associate yourself with people of good quality,
for it is better to be alone than to be in bad company"
~ Booker T. Washington

Another way to make sure that you are in an emotionally healthy relationship is to observe whether the person respects your basic rights in the relationship. These rights are:
- The right to emotional support
- The right to be heard by the other person and to be politely responded to
- The right to have your own view, even if your view is different

- The right to have your feelings and experiences acknowledged as real
- The right to live without accusations and blame
- The right to live without criticism and judgment
- The right to encouragement
- The right to feel safe from emotional and physical threat
- The right to live free from angry outbursts and rage
- The right to be called by no name that devalues you
- The right to be respectfully asked rather than ordered
- The right to have your work and your interests spoken of with respect
- The right to receive a sincere apology for any jokes that you find offensive

You may find that a member of your support team isn't a person. By this, I am referring to emotional support and service animals. It is astonishing to see how many people who suffer from a disability have animals that have been trained to help them. Guide dogs for the blind are the most obvious example.

Service animals have also been trained to help people with physical challenges, such as providing balance and support, assisting people in order to help them stand, and there are service dogs who are taught how to retrieve personal items for those who lack motor skills.

Emotional support animals are trained to help people with a myriad of problems, such as PTSD (post-traumatic stress disorder), seizure detection, diabetes support, and emotional support to help with depression or anxiety issues.

These are only some of the examples of a growing list of ways that animals are being trained to support people. If you think an emotional support or service animal may be helpful for you, I strongly suggest you look into getting one.

When I got my guide dog, Orbit, he literally changed my life. Not just as a guide dog, but also as a companion, a 'best friend' who helps me immensely while I socialize with others.

Every time we go out, even if it is just around the block, we meet new 'friends'. Since I teamed with Orbit, he has been with me every day—guiding me, playing with me, soliciting attention from me—and he has displayed more devotion to me than any person ever could. He has given me the confidence that allows us to go anywhere and overcome any obstacle. Now that is a great supporter!

One unpleasant area regarding service and emotional support animals that I would like to address, is the growing number of negative news stories about people who are taking their house pets into public areas and claiming they are service animals. Not only dogs, but snakes, pigs, chickens, cats, and birds. Anyone can go online and order a vest for their pet, claiming it is a service animal.

One story that comes to mind, is a passenger who took her miniature pig on a commercial flight. She claimed it was an emotional support animal, even though it was not trained for this purpose. The pig got loose in the cabin and made a real mess!

It is becoming more and more difficult for airlines, restaurants, retail stores, and hotels to distinguish a customer being assisted by a legitimately trained service animal from someone who has simply put a service vest on a pet. People who run a business are legally restricted from asking certain questions about an individual's disability or why the animal is required. For this reason, some businesses are clamping down on their policy of allowing any animals into their facilities.

A service animal goes through months, if not years, of extensive training. Each is certified and licensed to perform the demanding tasks that enable the disabled person to function comfortably in all aspects of their lives. These animals are painstakingly taught how to behave in public.

When irresponsible individuals take unruly house pets in public places, claiming they are service animals, all animal handlers suffer from the 'bad rap' of just a few. In addition, those impostors are acting in violation of the Americans with Disabilities Act.

Please, for the sake of those of us who rely on these important helpers, do not throw a vest on Fido and take him out claiming he is a service animal. You could ruin it for those of us who depend on these incredible companions and guides.

Regardless of where you find your support team, whether they are two-legged or four-legged, it is critical that you have a strong one. Today, you have more opportunities than ever to build a support team. Whether you choose family, friends, a support group, clergy, volunteer organizations, profess-ional counselors, life coaches, or clubs, a pet, a service animal—or any combination of these—there is a treasure trove of wonderful supporters out there waiting to help you. All you need to do is ask.

Chapter 7
Helping Kids Acquire Resiliency Skills

We may not be able to prepare the future for our children,
but we can at least prepare our children for the future."
~ Franklin D. Roosevelt

Young people today face more challenges and experience more temptations than we can possibly imagine. Not only do they need to deal with traditional issues, such as divorcing parents, problems at school, sibling rivalries, bullying, and illnesses; but they must also contend with a plethora of challenges that we never could have imagined.

With the saturation of smart phones, laptops, tablets, and any number of other internet-capable devices, a whole new cadre of issues faces our youth. With the advent of social media sites such as Facebook, Instagram and Snapchat, cyber-bullying can now reach out and strike our kids at any time of the day or night. Public embarrassment and teasing is considered the norm.

With just a click of a button, kids can view porn sites. Teens using drugs has risen to an all-time high—with easy access not only to marijuana, but also to stronger, more dangerous drugs such as methamphetamine and heroin.

Most schools today require hours and hours of home-work, which keeps kids 'wound up tight' with anxiety and depression. So it is no surprise that kids are finding it more and more difficult to successfully navigate the rough waters of adolescence. They are being faced with having to make adult decisions without the emotional skills to handle the consequences of those decisions.

This creates even more chaos in their lives. Issues that are minor irritants to adults often seem completely over-whelming to children. Neurological researchers have discovered that the frontal lobe of the human brain, the portion of the brain that is responsible for executive functioning, is not fully developed until the age of 24 or 25. The frontal lobe gives a person the ability to 'play the movie forward'. Fortunately, in spite of this discovery, research shows that kids can learn how to ask themselves the question, "If I do this, what will happen?" And if they make a wrong decision, possibly even one with dire consequences, they are capable of 'bouncing back.'

It's never too early to teach kids resiliency skills. If you are in a position to mentor kids as a parent, caregiver, teacher, coach, etc., you have an excellent opportunity to help turn struggling kids into resilient adults by teaching them skills that they can utilize for life.

> "Train up a child in the way he should go;
> even when he is old he will not depart from it."
> ~ Ephesians 6:4

Before we dive too deeply into the specifics of helping young people deal with challenges and how to thrive in spite of them, let's look at the signs of traumatized children and/or depressed children.

Some 'red flag' behaviors that indicate children are suffering from depression, trauma or both are:
- Retreating to their room
- A fear of attending school
- Rarely laughing
- Giving up their prized possessions
- Personalizing benign statements
- Displaying low energy
- Difficulty getting out of bed
- Feeling hopeless or helpless

- Losing interest in friends and activities that previously gave them joy
- Lacking concentration
- Struggling to overcome negative thoughts
- Sleep and appetite changes
- Self-loathing
- Anxiety about situations that previously were not a problem
- More irritable, short-tempered or aggressive
- Concentration problems
- Unexplained aches and pains

Children facing serious negative issues often have difficulty in school and isolate themselves from others. If they develop post-traumatic stress disorder (PTSD), they will repeatedly re-experience the traumatic ordeal in the form of flashbacks, memories, nightmares, or frightening thoughts, especially when they are exposed to events or objects that remind them of the trauma. PTSD has become a significant disorder for young people who have suffered any kind of trauma—death of a loved one, surviving an accident in which a friend died, being involved in a car accident, living in a household of continual chaos such as verbal and physical abuse.

If you observe a child who has any of these symptoms, put safety measures in place; including hiding anything that they can use to harm themselves (razors, scissors, sharp pencils, ropes, etc.). Give them the crisis hotline number in case they feel suicidal and encourage them to have a 'safe person' that they can contact. By all means, get them professional help. A licensed therapist can guide them through the problematic issues and teach them the tools they need to overcome the problem. A psychiatrist or physician can determine whether medication is warranted.

Several years ago, researcher Michael Rutter, defined six different risk factors that resulted from chronic family adversities. These included: severe marital discord, maternal psychiatric disorder, overcrowding or a large family, paternal criminality, low socio-economic status, and foster placement. Rutter observed that children who were exposed to a single risk factor seemed to adjust as well as children who were not exposed to any risk factor. But, children who were burdened with four or more risk factors increased their likelihood of a psychiatric disorder tenfold.

When children grow up in a family that is unsupportive; that is, one which provided very little warmth, acceptance and affection, they need someone—at least one person—to give them unconditional positive regard. This person can provide the kudos that children need to overcome their traumatic world and thrive in spite of it.

Research also shows that children who are traumatized and have 'overcome' have somehow acquired positive attributes to help them overcome their challenges. Many children who grew up in violent situations—but were skilled academically and were socially engaging—were able to use their positive experiences to help them overcome the turmoil that they experienced at home. Those who were encouraged by their teachers, supported by their friends, and welcomed by their friends' families developed a sense of mastery. In spite of childhood traumas, many of these children have grown up and embraced challenging careers. It's the encouragement of at least one person that has helped these traumatized children thrive. Those who have been successful refuse to label themselves as victims and they do not define themselves by their past.

One example of this is a study by Dr. Emmy Werner. Dr. Werner conducted a longitudinal study of native Hawaiians, which provided an encouraging case study of resilience. She wrote a book about her study, which was entitled '*Overcoming the Odds*'. Werner followed this group of islanders from late adolescence into middle age. The study consisted of 505 people born in 1955, on the island of Kauai. About half of these participants were born into poverty. Many of them grew up in homes where there was alcoholism, rage, and abuse. Werner observed that victim-theory would have predicted that by the time these children reached their twenties, they would have simply sunk into a swamp of crime and unemployment. But one-third never seemed to sink at all: they did well in school, began promising careers, and defined themselves as capable and competent adults.

The children who escaped serious harm were those who had positive attributes and were encouraged by others. They exhibited personalities that drew others toward them. They had hobbies, interests and talents that they were proud of. Many of these children had a teacher (or teachers) who believed in them. Or they had 'parent substitutes'—such as grandparents or older brothers and sisters. They had a support system that recognized, valued and rewarded their strengths, talents and abilities,

Another study by Dr. Norman Garmezy, noted that protective factors seem to fall into three general categories:

- Qualities of the child
- Characteristics of the family
- Support from outside the family

These studies show us that, as long as children have someone who believes in them, they can thrive in spite of any trauma that they are facing. There are ways in which we can instill protective factors in children. One way is to help children develop skills or activities in which they can shine, such as reading skills, drawing, or learning to play a sport. Noticing and encouraging your children to do the things in which they excel, creates self-confidence. As children recognize their positive attributes, they are able to dispute the negative thoughts that sometimes plague them. Helping your children come up with a list of positive characteristics about themselves gives them the power to reject what bullies may say about them.

Be honest with your children. Don't give them false confidence by telling them how great they are at everything. There will come a time when they will reach a point in their lives, that they know your words are untrue. Making children feel that they are good at everything does not prepare them for adulthood. As a matter of fact, constantly telling your children that they are good at everything, can ultimately make them feel entitled. Or, once they are adults, feel devastated when they realize they had been told they were incredible at something and clearly they are not.

Developing closeness, increasing positive affirmations, and facilitating communication, helps to solidify truly supportive family relationships. Families can strengthen their relationships by paying close attention to what makes them a family such as: beliefs, values, emotional warmth, support, organization, and communication. Parenting plays an important role in whether children feel confident or unconfident. There are three basic types of parenting: authoritarian, permissive, and authoritative.

- *Authoritarian parents* have rigid boundaries. Children from this type of family do not feel heard or understood and they don't feel confident enough to make decisions on their own.
- *Permissive parents* allow their children to make adult decisions of which they are not yet capable of doing. These children often feel that their parents do not care about them. They often struggle with decisions because they fear they will make a bad choice.
- *Authoritative parents* set boundaries— but also allow their children to make some of their own decisions within those boundaries. This gives children the ability to learn that bad behavior creates negative consequences. These children are most likely to feel that they have a voice, that they are heard and that they can disagree with their parents as long as it is respectfully communicated.

Parents often forget that their children are not supposed to meet their needs, rather parents are supposed to meet the needs of their children. Children come into the world with their own, unique personalities, and our responsibility is to guide them and teach them:

Honesty/Accountability

How can you expect your children to be honest with you if you lie to them? If you say you are going to do something, follow through with it. If you are unable to follow-through, apologize for it. Teach your kids to say what they mean and mean what they say. When you can't do something that you said you would do, take ownership of it. This models to your children that it is ok to be imperfect and that you do not expect them to be perfect either. Teach your children that 'work comes before play'. This can start at a very early age. ("Is your room picked up? Then, let's go to the park.") Teamwork teaches accountability to children: cleaning the house, working in the yard, or completing a project together.

Spirituality

Numerous studies have demonstrated that when children believe there is a power greater than themselves, they feel a responsibility to honor themselves and others. When children and adults embrace spirituality during times of stress, they often feel a tremendous sense of relief.

Respect/Empathy

If young children are taught to examine how others may feel in a given situation, they can carry that empathetic skill into adulthood. One way to do this when your child tells you about something that happened to a friend at school ask, "I wonder how he felt when that happened?" This gives children the opportunity to step out of their own shoes and to see it from another person's perspective. Getting your children involved in a charity or an activity like an 'adopt a family' program at Thanksgiving or Christmas, will encourage them to be grateful for what they have and to empathize with those who struggle. These examples help kids learn 'people skills', skills such as listening to a person when they are troubled, helping those in need, being kind to others.

Respect toward elders and how to address those with titles such as Miss, Mrs., Mr., or Dr. seem to have disappeared with today's youth. Much of this is the fault of parenting. You must teach your children that they are not equal to those in authority. By doing this, you will set them up for success in the real world. They will need to be respectful toward their managers, police officers etc. Make sure that you model this behavior. How you handle a situation with one of their teachers can be a great example. Many times your children may have a teacher that they do not like. But, how you handle this situation can make a huge difference in how they deal with an 'impossible' person in their future. Unless your children are being grossly misunderstood, bullied or overtly slighted, they need to learn that there are people in this world whom they may not necessarily agree with but, who are to be respected because of their position.

Consequences

How can a child learn how to navigate life if a parent rushes in and fixes it? Do you buy them a new cell phone every time they break theirs? Do you give them an allowance and teach them the concept of money, or do you simply give them money each month without holding them responsible for what they do with it? Do you simply hand them money for whatever you think they need? Do you rescue your children from their problems? Do you take their lunch to school for them when they forget it? Or finish an assignment for them? Or pay for their speeding tickets? When parents 'rescue' their children from their own behavior, it enables children to be helpless. When parents fail to enforce consequences for behaviors that their children have chosen, it teaches them how to manipulate others to get what they want.

Kids are much more likely to become resilient when they understand that there are consequences for their behavior.

Psychologists observe that children will become ir-responsible adults if parents lie for them, make excuses for their behavior, accept responsibility for their kids' mistakes, refuse to believe that one of their children is guilty of what they are being accused of, fight their battles, tolerate and excuse their abusive or unacceptable behavior, or routinely let them get away with not doing things that they are expected to do.

When parents fail to prepare their children for adulthood they set their kids up for failure; failure in relationships because they have never worked hard for anything, failure in business because they haven't been taught how to do a job well, and failure in life because they are oblivious to how to set a goal and to follow through with it.

Mark Gregson, a Christian author, speaker, and CEO of *Heartlight Ministries*, gives five important rules for parenting:

Rules should be relevant
They should match the age of your child. What may be a good rule for an 8-year-old may not be a rule that will work for a 16-year-old. An example would be a practical time for bed. Sending an 8-year-old to bed at 8pm makes sense but for a 16-year-old it would be ridiculous. Good rules need to be flexible. Rules need to change as your child ages. Your goal, as a parent, is to allow your child to become more independent and less dependent upon you.

Rules should be attainable
When parents set up unrealistic rules, children often give up and become oppositional. If, for example, your children are not capable of getting A's and you punish them for failing to reach that goal, you are setting them up for failure. Before you know it, they may convince themselves "I'm not good enough." A more realistic goal for some kids might be "if you get a D, you lose X, Y and Z."

Rules should be beneficial
Ask yourself these questions: will this rule help my children to build self-esteem? Will it help them to be more responsible and more trustworthy? Will these rules benefit my children by preparing them for adulthood?

Rules should make sense
Many parents forget that there are some rules that don't have a logical purpose. The freedom to express who they are helps young people to build healthy self-esteem. So, growing their hair long, coloring it, or wearing an earring may be just fine. If, however, their choices put them in harm's way; i.e., dressing like a thug. Or if the choice could prevent them from getting a

professional job someday; i.e., tattoos and body piercings that they cannot cover. Then you must draw the line. You cannot allow your teens self-expression to hamper their future success. There should be a logical reason for every rule. If you can't explain why the rule is important (because I said so doesn't count), then the rule needs to be tossed.

Rules should come from a place of love

If you set strict rules and expect them to be enforced but you lack a relationship with your children, they will most likely rebel. Your children need to be heard, understood and loved. They are faced with many choices every day and some of their choices may not be wise ones. But they need to know that your love is unconditional and that your rules come from a place of wanting to protect them from harm and to prepare them for real life.

What produces success? That's relatively easy to answer: hard work, persistence, tenacity, great effort and resiliency. We see it in business, in relationships, and even in nature. Watch a baby bird as it attempts to hatch from its egg. The struggle of it breaking its shell is imperative for its survival. Without the struggle, the bird would die. And while children shouldn't have to struggle to live, they are more likely to be successful if they have to put forth effort. When they don't work hard, they aren't as likely to excel in business or in relationships. Our job as parents is to prepare our children for real life, to teach our children as many life lessons as possible, and to give them the tools that they need to be resilient... no matter what life throws at them.

"The family should be a closely knit group. The home should be a self-contained shelter of security; a kind of school where life's basic lessons are taught; and a kind of church where God is honored; a place where wholesome recreation and simple pleasures are enjoyed."
~ Billy Graham

Chapter 8
A Healthy Body Improves Resiliency

If you want to be resilient enough to go out there and slay 'dragons' day in and day out, it is crucial to have a healthy body. It only stands to reason that the better you feel, the better equipped you will be to deal with whatever life hands you. If you are on top of your game physically, you will be on top of your game mentally.

While I certainly do not profess to be an expert in the wellness field, I would like to share with you some of the daily activities and habits that have helped to keep me healthy and happy. If you need assistance in any of these areas, I encourage you to seek professional assistance.

Look at your body as a three-legged stool:
- Healthy diet
- Regular exercise
- Adequate sleep

Nutritious diet

It requires a lot of energy to slay 'dragons' every day. A healthy diet will help equip you with that energy. We Americans are both blessed and cursed to enjoy a wider selection of food than any other civilization—ever. And that is good. Unfortunately, though, with all these choices come just as many opportunities to make bad choices. But always remember that we have the option to make good ones.

There has been so much written about the topic of diet and nutrition that, over the years, these books and articles could fill a library. It is far beyond the intent of this book to delve into this complex and ever changing subject. Of the thousands of studies, guidelines and programs that there are, they all have a similar theme; you need to eat a well-balanced, nutritious diet. This will require some research on your part, as you need to do what is best for you and your body. Beyond the books, internet searches and programs available, you may consider consulting a dietitian or nutritionist. The main point I want to make is that by having a healthy, nutritious diet, you are more likely to possess the physical strength to handle any adversity.

"And God said, "Behold, I have given you every
plant yielding seed that is on the face of all the earth,
and every tree with seed in its fruit.
You shall have them for food."
~ Genesis 1:29

There are some dietary changes that you can make that will help you. For example, when you shop at the grocery store, try to choose the majority of your food from the sections located along the perimeter such as produce (fruits and vegetables), meat, bakery and dairy sections. Here you will find the 'whole' foods in their most natural form. These foods are easier for your body to digest and better for your overall health than the processed foods that are located in the center aisles. Processed foods often provide little or no nutritional value and are typically high in calories. Naturally, it would be easy to avoid them, if they didn't taste so good. High sugar cereals, cookies, candies and snack cakes are difficult to pass up.

Take Twinkies, for instance. Those delicious, cream filled cakes can't be that bad for you, can they? Peruse the ingredient list and you will quickly change your mind. There are 37 ingredients in a Twinkie. A few of them don't look too bad— flour, sugar and eggs. On the other hand, some of these ingredients will make you think twice before you take your next bite—*sodium acid pyrophosphate, mono calcium phosphate, soy protein, mono and diglycerides, sodium stearoyl lactylate, calcium and sodium caseinate, triglycerides, polysorbate 60, and sorbic acid.*

Yuck! For me, avoiding processed foods entirely is something that is not likely to happen in the near future. The key, though, is this: all things in moderation. It is snack time now, but instead of cookies, I think I will have an apple.

The United States Department of Health and Human Services recommends that you have at least nine servings of fruits and vegetables every day. I do not know about you, but I am lucky if I get four. During my presentations, I often ask the audience how many of them get their nine servings each day. According to my very unscientific results, I would say that less than 10% indicate they do. (To be quite honest, I think this number is high. I really believe that some of these people may simply be trying to impress their colleagues.) To help me compensate for the vitamins and nutrients that I do not receive through my fruits and vegetables, I have implemented two strategies. First, in order to increase my fruit and vegetable intake, I endeavor to eat at least one fruit with breakfast, one vegetable with lunch, a fruit snack in the afternoon and at least one vegetable with dinner. Secondly, I take a vitamin and nutrient supplement called 'Juice Plus'. Since I started on this regimen several years ago, I have had more energy throughout the day and I have fewer incidents of cold, flu, and sinus infections.

Fast foods are another area in which you need to be careful. It is, unfortunately, a fact of life that many of us eat fast foods. But be careful! Sure, the foods are fast and cheap, but they are not nutritious. The key to keeping fast foods from destroying your diet and your health is: (a) what you select, and (b) how large the serving size is.

Most fast food chains now offer a healthy alternative so you are not forced to choose their high-calorie, high-fat selections. It is up to you — a bacon cheeseburger, large fries and milkshake... or a Cobb salad and a bottle of water.

Does that mean you can never have a bacon cheeseburger? Of course not. But again, it is imperative to do everything in moderation.

"The more you eat, the less flavor; the less you eat,
the more flavor."
~ Chinese Proverb

As important as what you eat and drink may be, it is just as important to be aware of what you do not eat and drink.

Start with meal portions. Even though it flies in the face of what your mom or grandma may have taught you, do not feel obligated to eat everything on your plate. This is especially true when you visit a restaurant. Make take-home bags a part of your dining experience. Stretching that dinner into two meals will do wonders for your waistline, and your budget.

Keep your snacking at home to a minimum. Just because you have a package of chocolate chip cookies does not mean that you need to carry the entire box to your recliner and watch TV. If you do that, you may be mortified when you look down and see that you have inhaled all the cookies before your favorite show is half over. Instead, just grab three or four cookies and leave the package in the pantry. You will savor the limited supply much more, and you'll be far less tempted to wolf down all of the cookies without even thinking about it.

Another area to look at regarding your food intake is whether you drink alcohol. Excessive drinking can negatively affect your health in many ways. Many studies indicate that a glass of wine is beneficial to your health. But, if you cannot limit your intake to a drink or two, it may be time to seek professional help.

"Wine is a mocker, strong drink a brawler,
and whoever is led astray by it is not wise."
~ Proverbs 20:1

Gluten-free diets are all the rage now. You are most likely seeing many more items on your grocery shelves and finding that many of your favorite restaurants are now offering gluten-free options. You most likely have observed gluten-free restaurants pop up, especially in California (where else?).

Before you dismiss gluten-free diets as the latest fad, let's look at the facts.

Wheat has been so genetically modified over the last fifty years, it's DNA is not even close to that of the original wheat product that your grandparents served at their dinner table. Once wheat enters your digestive tract, the gluten, (which is the binding that helps the wheat stick together) gets sticky, which makes it difficult to digest. This can cause a whole host of problems. I have heard several stories about people who have benefited from removing wheat from their diets, even though they did not have a food sensitivity to it. This is something that is worth considering. It is shocking to see how many products have wheat in them. Wheat is even in many candies—including Twizzlers!

Regular exercise

You need to be physically sturdy to be resilient. The benefits of a regular exercise program are well documented. Exercise provides you with more strength and endurance. It helps you to maintain a healthy body weight and it gives you more energy. Lifting weights or performing other resistance training builds and strengthens your muscles. Aerobic exercise releases endorphins, which in turn, reduces stress, anxiety and depression. Not to mention, it just makes you feel better. Exercise not only helps your heart; it helps your brain.

It is no secret that the human body needs regular activity to stay healthy. The key to success is to determine what level of exercise is right for you. For some people, a brisk walk around the block does the job. Others need a more vigorous program. It all depends on your genetics, your gender, your age, and your overall health. You may want to consult a personal trainer to help you establish the best program for you.

Do not make the mistake of thinking that an effective exercise program means two hours at the gym—five or six days a week. It does not. Your program may start out as a thirty-minute walk, three days a week. The important thing is to just do something. Find an activity that you enjoy—swimming, yoga, walking on a treadmill, biking, weightlifting or running—

anything that will keep you interested and active. You may be a person who is more motivated when you work out at a gym. Although, many people are more comfortable working out in the privacy of their home. Whatever you do, just do it!

If you are searching for workout ideas, your smartphone or the internet have hundreds of apps and programs that can help you get started. So, pick up your Smartphone and start looking for an exercise program that will get your blood flowing.

A nifty trick that may motivate you to work out more often, is to electronically monitor your daily activity. There are any number of devices that you can purchase to help with this. My wife, Kristi, recently started wearing a device called a Fitbit. It is very small, about the size of a bottle cap, and it is to be worn all day. (Apparently it is waterproof. Kristi ran it through the washer by mistake—and it still works!) The device counts your steps, the distance you've covered, and the calories you have burned. It even has a sleep tracker. Unfortunately, it is not user-friendly for blind people; but there are products available on smart phones that are.

While on the topic of working out, don't forget to exercise your brain as well as your body. Current neuroscience research shows that exercising your brain improves your reasoning ability, sharpens your memory, increases your problem solving skills, and facilitates your decision-making. These improved skills reduce stress and help you adapt to changes much faster, thus making you more resilient.

According to an article in the November, 2007 Harvard Business Review, "...the brain's anatomy, neural networks and cognitive abilities can be strengthened and improved through experiences and interactions with the environment."

There are a number of websites that can help you test—and consequently improve—your cognitive ability skills, including memory, attention and problem solving. One I like is *lumosity.com*. This site allows you to set up a personal account. You can test and monitor your progress and compare your results with others around the world. The site is designed to be fun, using games and other tools to help you improve cognition.

One very important factor regarding your physical and mental health that cannot be ignored is genetics. To a large degree your weight, propensity to illness, life expectancy, mental health, and many other traits are determined by your family of origin. Some researchers believe that heredity is almost as significant as lifestyle. Keep this in mind when you are setting up diet and exercise programs. Some people are blessed with good genetics; others not so much. You will need to factor in your genetics when developing your program (i.e.: food intake, exercise duration and frequency, etc.) If you are eating a healthy diet and exercising regularly but still cannot seem to lose those last ten or twenty pounds, don't sweat it. Maybe your genetic code is pre-programmed for those extra pounds. Rather than stressing about it, it may be time to become comfortable with your current weight and start working on some new, positive goals in other areas of your life.

Adequate sleep

To slay those dragons by day, you need plenty of sleep at night. This critical leg of the three-legged stool for a healthy body is often overlooked, but it is just as important as diet and exercise. A person dealing with sleep deprivation can suffer from mental and physical problems. If you are not getting adequate sleep, your body and mind cannot operate at its peak performance. Experts say that we need seven to nine hours of sleep every night. In today's busy world, with work, family and other time commitments, we are all finding a full night of sleep more and more difficult.

If you are having problems getting adequate sleep, here are some tips that may help.

Tip 1- Keep a regular sleep schedule.

It is imperative to get your body's sleep/wake cycles (circadian rhythm) in sync. Try to go to sleep and wake up at the same time every day. This will give you quality sleep time and help you to feel more refreshed. Yes, this also applies for weekends.

- Set a regular bedtime. Pick a time when you start to naturally feel tired.

- If you need an alarm clock to wake up, you are probably not getting enough sleep. Try going to bed earlier or waking up later.
- If you get behind on your sleep, it is OK to take a short, power nap during the day. This will allow you to maintain your natural wake/sleep cycle. Limit the nap to the early afternoon and rest no more than thirty minutes.
- If you find yourself getting drowsy in the early evening, get off the couch and do something mildly active. Do some light chores, work on a hobby, or reorganize your closet. If you fall asleep in the early evening, you may wake up in the middle of the night and then you will most likely have difficulty falling back to sleep.

Tip 2- Regulate your sleep/wake cycle.

Melatonin is a naturally occurring hormone produced in the brain. This 'brain hormone' helps restore restful sleep. Because this cycle is controlled by light exposure, your brain should secrete more melatonin at night, which helps you sleep, and less melatonin during the day, which allows you to stay awake. Unfortunately, since the invention of electricity, the use of artificial light has wreaked havoc with our natural cycles. Hours spent in front of a TV, the computer screen, or a smartphone suppress the natural production of melatonin, thus making it more difficult to fall asleep. To reverse this phenomenon, try these suggestions:

- Spend twenty minutes each day outside, allowing your body to absorb the sunshine.
- Open the curtains in your home and office to get more sunshine.
- Turn off your TV, computer or smartphone a couple of hours before you go to bed. Not only does the screen reduce melatonin production, viewing it can stimulate your mind.

- Do something relaxing to help you get ready for sleep, like reading, listening to an audio book or music.
- Make sure your room is dark. Turn off all the lights, cover windows with black out shades. The darker your room is, the better you will sleep.
- Take melatonin before you go to bed. It is sold over the counter. It is inexpensive and it will help you sleep throughout the night. And if you wake, melatonin can help you fall back to sleep.

Tip 3- Make your bedroom sleep ready.

Create a conducive environment for sleep. Doing this will allow your body to understand that it is time for a restful night's slumber.

- Make sure you are sleeping on a 'Goldilocks' mattress, not too firm, not too soft. It needs to be just right.
- Your pillow choice is just as important as your mattress. Make sure it is not too fluffy or to flat, too firm, or too soft.
- Keep your room cool. People tend to sleep better in a cool (65 to 75 degrees) well-ventilated room. If a room is too warm or too cool, it can affect the quality of your sleep.
- Use an air filter, a sound machine or a phone sleep app to provide white noise. This will help block out annoying noises such as barking dogs, blaring sirens or loud neighbors.
- Limit your bed time to sleep time. If you turn your bed into a home office or an entertainment center, your brain will not associate it as a place of rest. Do your TV viewing, web surfing or other electronic gadget activity from a bedroom chair or in another room. Consistently practice this so that your brain associates that the bed is only for sleeping.

- Do not allow your pets to sleep in bed with you. Make them sleep in their own beds on the floor. They will get used to it.

Tip 4- Watch what you eat /drink before bedtime.

It is important to be aware of what you put into your body before your bedtime. Paying close attention to this can mean the difference between a good night's sleep or a restless one.

- Avoid large meals or snacking at night. Eat earlier in the evening. Consume a light dinner. Stay away from spicy, acidic or rich foods because they can cause heartburn or other stomach problems and interfere with a good night's sleep.
- Stay away from alcoholic beverages before bed. It is a myth that a 'nightcap' will help you to sleep better. It may help you to fall asleep faster, but having a drink usually causes you to wake in the middle of the night. And a bonus for skipping the nightcap is waking without a headache. Instead, you will wake feeling refreshed and ready for the day.
- Limit your caffeine intake. Caffeine can remain in your system for up to twelve hours and thus can prevent you from getting a good night's sleep. This means coffee, tea, most sodas, energy drinks, and yes, even chocolate.
- In the evening, do not drink too many liquids of any type, including water. Cutting down on your liquid intake will reduce the number of nightly trips you need to make to the bathroom.
- If you smoke-quit. Nicotine is both a sedative and a stimulant. So, as the night progresses, if you are addicted to nicotine, you may suffer from nicotine withdrawal, which will wake you because your brain tells you that it is time for a smoke. This will only exacerbate your sleep problems.

Tip 5- Get some exercise.

If you exercise on a regular basis, as recommended earlier in this chapter, you will sleep better.

- Exercise during the day. Physical activity too late at night will invigorate the body, which makes it difficult to fall to sleep.
- Light activity before bedtime, such as mild yoga or gentle stretching, will encourage sleep. This is better than just sitting on the couch before you go to bed.

Tip 6- Clear your mind.

It is difficult, if not impossible, to fall asleep if you are worrying about your problems of the day. Employ some simple tactics to help you get to sleep or to fall back to sleep if you wake during the night.

- Try some relaxation techniques, such as slow, deep breathing, progressive muscle relaxation, or visualizing that you are in a quiet, calm place, such as the beach or the mountains.
- Do not stress if you wake up. This will simply intensify the problem. Remind yourself that you are getting a good deal of rest by simply lying there and relaxing.
- If you are awake for fifteen to thirty minutes, it may help you relax by getting up and moving around. Then, return to bed and do something non-stimulating, such as reading a book. To keep from stimulating the brain, avoid electronic screens of any kind.
- Keep a notepad on your nightstand. Then, if you are worrying about something, like suddenly remembering an important task that you need to complete, or even have an epiphany—make a quick note of it. After you make that note, your brain will give itself permission to stop thinking about it and will allow you to go back to sleep.

- Come up with a relaxing mind game to calm your brain from the worries of the day. One example is the alphabet game. Think of a topic (cities, states, countries, sports teams, movies, books you are reading, etc.) and use every letter of the alphabet for the category that you choose. Take your time and be thorough. There is no time clock and no winner, except you... when you fall to sleep.

If you have tried all of these tips and you are still having trouble sleeping, you can find a lot of information on the Internet, and many books on the subject.

Still struggling? If so, it may be time to see your family physician, who may then refer you to a sleep specialist who can perform a scientifically monitored sleep study and help you get to the root of your problem. Regardless of how you do it, getting a good night's rest can literally change your life.

> "A good laugh and a long sleep are the best cures
> in the doctor's book."
>
> ~ Irish Proverb

And finally... Personal grooming

After you get your body in good shape and are enjoying a good night's sleep, don't forget to add that final, vital touch. Work on your appearance before you go out to meet the masses. Take a shower, shave, comb your hair, brush your teeth and put on clean clothes. We are not refugees here, folks. This only takes a few minutes. Taking the time to do this, will demonstrate to the world that you are confident and professional. We are people on a mission to accomplish great things. Let us look the part.

Now you are totally and completely ready to go out there and 'slay those dragons'!

Chapter 9
Stomp Out Negative Thinking

"We can complain because rose bushes have thorns, or rejoice because thorn bushes have roses."

~ Abraham Lincoln

In Chapter 4, we addressed the fact that resilient people exhibit positive attitudes. One of the primary challenges that individuals face in maintaining a positive attitude is negative thinking. When your brain is clouded with all of the reasons something will not work, or if you believe that you are incapable of accomplishing a task, you cannot perform at your maximum capacity. Once you effectively replace negative thoughts with positive ones, you are on the road to successfully accomplish your goals. Remember this important maxim: thoughts are random; feelings are a choice.

The next time negative thoughts creep into your mind—thoughts like "I am not smart enough." "I am not good enough." "I am a failure."—fight the negative thoughts. Talk back to them. There are several ways in which you can effectively stomp on negative thoughts. Let's start with a popular method called **distraction** and **disputation**.

Distraction

The first thing you need to do when you have negative thoughts is to distract your current mindset immediately so you can get off the negative road that your brain is running down. There is no reason to stay on this thoroughfare any longer than you have to. It will only make it more difficult to get back on the positive thinking highway. Distraction is a process that gives you unlimited choices. Here are just a few examples:

- Stop the negative thought by doing a brief activity. Do something pro-active that will stop you from thinking that negative thought—right now!
- Do some deep breathing exercises
- Concentrate on relaxing your mind and lowering your heart rate.
- Stand up and perform some light stretching exercises, concentrating on each muscle group as you stretch.
- Go for a short walk around the block, or around the office. Focus your attention on noticing what you see—objects, activities and people.
- Pet your dog, cat or another favorite pet. If you are an animal lover, nothing takes your mind off of your problems like interacting with a pet.
- If you are unable to stop the negative thoughts with a brief activity, shift your attention to an activity of a longer duration.
- Read a novel or a favorite magazine.
- Pull out your smartphone and peruse the current events. Get lost in the latest YouTube postings. Listen to some upbeat music. Look at some personal photos.
- Get some exercise. Listen to music as you walk on the treadmill or lift weights. Physical activity typically puts individuals in a better mood.
- If you are at home, get busy. Escape your problems by sorting clothes, doing the dishes, vacuuming the living room, or organizing your office.

Adjust your timing, when appropriate

On the other hand, if the negative thought is one that you clearly need to deal with, but you are not at a place or a time in which you can devote the attention it requires, schedule a time to deal with it. Jot it down on your 'things to do' list, make a note on your smartphone reminder app, or put it on a sticky note—use whatever organizational system that works for you. Be sure that you schedule time to contemplate this issue during one of your peak periods. (See the section later in this chapter on daily rhythms.) After you have noted when you will deal with the negative issue, allow your brain to let it go.

If the issue absolutely, positively cannot wait another minute, then excuse yourself and go to a private place where you can logically think the problem through without distractions.

Disputation

Most of the time, negative thoughts are erroneous. Sure, we all have challenges, but they are just natural functions of living in this world. Combat negative thoughts with disputation, which is challenging your beliefs. Learn how to argue with yourself.

Try asking and answering for yourself these questions:

- Was there a reason for the adversity or negative thought that has nothing to do with you? Perhaps the adversity or negative thought was not your fault. Let's say, for example, that you received a negative performance review at work, even though you know your performance was good. Was there an external influence that predisposed your supervisor to write a poor review? Was she going through a difficult time in her life, such as a family problem, financial troubles, health issues, issues with her boss, etc.? If the answer is yes, just chalk up the experience to bad timing. Note and date your disagreement regarding the review and then let it go.
- Was there something specific going on in your life at the time? Look and see if there was a specific event taking place in your life that may have caused the adversity or negative thought. Were you having family problems, financial issues, health woes, etc.? If so, it is important that you address the root problem, which can certainly help you correct the secondary issue. In the case of the

negative performance review, fixing your primary issue will most likely improve your performance at work.

- Is there a less catastrophic way to look at the situation? Many people tend to catastrophize personal situations. They over-react, make mountains out of molehills and assume the worst possible outcome. Be objective and keep events in perspective. If you find you are unrealistically assessing a situation, it may be helpful to 'play the movie forward'. Will the outcome be as damaging as you originally thought? In the example of the poor performance review, assuming there were no unique circumstances involved, how severe can the repercussions of a poor work review actually be? It is highly unlikely that you will lose your job because of one poor review. Let the negative event serve as a warning to you, so that you will make positive changes before the next review. (For more on over-reacting, see the 'Keep difficult times in perspective' segment in the 'Resiliency Triangle-Attitude' chapter.)
- Is there evidence to support your negative thought? Make sure that you have incontrovertible evidence that the situation causing the negative thought actually exists before you waste time and energy worrying about it. First, be a detective and investigate the situation, gather evidence and research your findings. Then, put the negative thought on the witness stand and question it just as a prosecuting attorney would. Was it really a poor review, or merely average? Are you being too hard on yourself? You may end up throwing the case out of court due to a lack of supporting evidence.
- Are there 'changeable' reasons for the situation? If the situation is 'changeable', put an action plan in place to change it. Let's say that after you work

through the disputation evaluation, you decide the belief is true. If it appears that there were no outside factors affecting the circumstance and there was nothing unusual happening in your life, then the evidence points to the fact that the situation is true. Therefore, in the example of the poor performance review, you need to come up with tools that will make you a better employee.

ะ

You may also want to employ the **SMART** goal setting model that we defined in chapter 5.

S- Specific goals

Improve your attendance. Upgrade your attitude. Complete your tasks on time. Be courteous and helpful to others.

M- Measure your productivity and success

Set numeric goals for hours worked, sales, client contacts, and any other performance measurements used in your business or career.

A- Achievable

Be realistic. You can't work 100 hours per week or make $1,000,000 in sales every month. It's a marathon, not a sprint.

R- Relevant

Will your goals really make you a better employee? Are they in line with your moral and ethical standards?

T- Timetable

Write down your plan. Record specific dates on which you plan to accomplish each item.

If there is absolutely nothing you can do to correct the situation, let go, let God, and trust the process. If the belief is destructive, it will negatively affect your mental and physical health. In the performance review example, let's say you are the manager of a Blockbuster store and the year is 2002. Your yearly evaluation is based on rentals, which are declining dramatically every quarter. This is due to the fact that customers are discovering the ease and convenience of streaming movies. The economic status of the video rental business is shaky. There is nothing you can do about this. It is unchangeable. Maybe it is time to update your résumé and send it to one of the relatively new internet companies that your customers have been recommending, like Amazon or Netflix.

For more information on distraction and disputation, read *Learned Optimism* by Martin E. P. Seligman, Ph.D.

> "We cannot change our past.
> We cannot change the fact that people act in a certain way.
> We cannot change the inevitable.
> The only thing we can do is play on the one string we have,
> and that is our attitude."
> ~ Chuck Swindoll

Another helpful concept in dealing with negative thoughts comes from Dr. Daniel Amen, a psychiatrist, medical researcher, and New York Times bestselling author. He defines automatic negative thinking as **ANT**s. He says that there are nine different ways that your thoughts lie to you and make situations seem worse than they are. They are:

- **Always/never thinking:** thinking words like always, never, no one, everyone, every time, everything.
- **Focusing on the negative**: seeing only the bad in a situation.
- **Fortune-telling:** predicting the worst possible outcome to a situation.
- **Mind-reading:** believing that you know what others are thinking, even though they haven't told you.
- **Thinking with your feelings:** believing negative feelings without questioning them.
- **Guilt beating:** thinking in words like should, must, ought or have to.
- **Labeling:** attaching a negative label to yourself or to someone else.

- **Personalizing:** investing innocuous events with personal meaning.
- **Blaming:** blaming someone else for your own problems.

Dr. Amen says that the best way to 'kill the **ANT**' is to talk back to it. Or, as we just talked about, dispute it.

I wish I had understood the theory of automatic negative thinking (ANT) when I lost my eyesight. I wasted a good deal of time ruminating about **ANT**s. One **ANT** that took a lot of my time was **always/never thinking**. Always and never thinking became a part-time job for me. There were times I truly felt that because of my blindness that I would not be able to accomplish anything worthwhile for the rest of my life. I believed I would never be able to enjoy playing a guitar, playing golf, snow skiing, riding a bike, or going to the movies. Saddened by the thought of never being able to take part in any of these activities, I spent many hours in a state of deep depression. If I had known how to kill the always/never **ANT**, I would not have wasted so much time feeling despondent about my perceived losses.

Another dangerous personal **ANT** was **fortune-telling.** I predicted a dire future for myself and my family. After all, what could a blind person do? Not very much, I thought. Well, I have since learned that I can accomplish just about anything I set my mind to. There are blind people in almost every profession that you can imagine—from attorneys to zookeepers, doctors to mechanics. They are engaged in every sport imaginable, from golfing to mountain climbing, running marathons to snow skiing. I used to say that, as a blind man, I could do anything that I wanted to do except drive a car. But now that self-driving cars are on the horizon, it may not be long before you see me behind the wheel of a car again.

Mind-reading was a powerful **ANT** that ruled my life. I was convinced that everyone I met was judging me. I believed they were thinking, "There is that poor blind guy who was in that terrible accident." I was sure they were thinking things like "what is he going to be able to do now?" "How can he ever be happy?" "How can a blind man be a good Dad or husband."

In those early days, I made the mistake of 'labeling'. 'Blind' became the primary identifier of who I was. I thought that I was the 'blind' husband; the 'blind' dad; the 'blind' son; the 'blind' brother; the 'blind' friend. This was negative thinking of perhaps the worst kind. When I labeled myself as blind, it immediately set the stage with a negative pre-qualification. I have since embraced the fact that I am a person who just happens to be blind. This is a much healthier mental place to be.

I now understand that whatever your situation, you cannot let other people set limits on what you can and cannot accomplish. You need to set the goals you wish to achieve, pursue them, and do not worry about what others think. Regardless of your limitations, it is up to you to set the bar—so set it high!

> "Things turn out best for the people
> who make the best of the way things turn out."
> ~ John Wooden

Rational Emotive Behavior Therapy

In the mid 1950s, Albert Ellis, PhD, developed a theory that he called Rational Emotive Behavioral Therapy or R.E.B.T. This theory is still practiced today by many psychologists. I appreciate the way in which Dr. Ellis defines this theory, because it is logical and easy to remember with a simple acronym: A-B-C-D, like this:

A. Activating experience. Example: Your wife fails to call you at the designated time.

B. Belief about or interpretation of the activating experience. You think, "My wife hasn't called, therefore she must be with someone else." "This is terrible." "I guess I am just not good enough."

C. Consequences of your emotional upset may be depression, sadness or anger.

D. Dispute the irrational ideas by asking questions; i.e., "Where is the evidence?" "Just because I haven't heard from her does not mean that she is with someone else." "She could have been held up in a meeting, her phone could have died or she may have simply forgotten to call."

ঙ্ক

On the topic of irrational ideas, be aware of what your thoughts are and recognize the irrational ones. Let's review a list of irrational ideas as defined by Dr. Ellis.

Irrational Idea No. 1: The idea that it is a dire necessity for you to be loved or approved of by virtually every significant other person in your community.

Irrational Idea No. 2: The idea that you should be thoroughly competent, adequate, and achieving in all possible aspects if you are to consider yourself worthwhile.

Irrational Idea No. 3: The idea that certain people are bad, wicked, or villainous and that they should be severely blamed and punished for their wickedness.

Irrational Idea No. 4: The idea that it is awful and catastrophic when things are not the way you would like them to be.

Irrational Idea No. 5: The idea that human unhappiness is externally caused and that people have little or no ability to control their sorrows and disturbances.

Irrational Idea No. 6: The idea that if something is, or may be, dangerous or fearsome, you should be terribly concerned about it and should keep dwelling on the possibility of it occurring.

Irrational Idea No. 7: The idea that it is easier to avoid than to face certain life difficulties.

Irrational Idea No. 8: The idea that you should be dependent upon others and need someone stronger than yourself to rely on.

Irrational Idea No. 9: The idea that your past history is an all-important determiner of your present behavior and that because something once strongly affected your life, that it should indefinitely have a similar effect.

Irrational Idea No. 10: The idea that you should become quite upset over other people's problems.

Irrational Idea No. 11: The idea that there is in-variably a right, precise, and perfect solution to human problems and that it is catastrophic if the perfect solution is not found.

Each morning when I open my eyes I say to myself: I, not events, have the power to make me happy or unhappy today. I can choose which it shall be. Yesterday is dead. Tomorrow hasn't arrived yet. I have just one day, today, and I'm going to be happy in it.

~ Groucho Marx

Be aware of your daily rhythms

Throughout the day, the human body has natural emotional and energy rhythms, known as the Basic Rest Activity Cycle (BRAC). This concept was proposed by Nathaniel Kleitman, a physiologist and sleep researcher. These rhythmic peaks and valleys are different for each individual. Know your daily rhythms, and plan your day accordingly. Schedule the optimal time to handle difficult tasks when you are at your peak times, both emotionally and physically. Your problem solving skills, decision making abilities, and negotiating talents will be their sharpest during these times. Save mundane tasks and routine activities for the times of the day when you are at your lowest operational effectiveness.

In general, the following BRAC rules apply:

- We tend to start the morning with low levels of energy and attitude. No surprise here. As we get further into the morning, and finish our first cup of coffee, our energy levels increase and our attitudes improve. For most of us, first thing in the morning is not the best time of day to try to accomplish anything except making coffee and eating breakfast.
- Most people hit their low energy and attitude levels around 4:00 in the morning and 4:00 in the afternoon. You know what it is like; you wake at 4:00 am with some serious problem that you can

see no way out of. Later in the morning, after you have had that second cup of coffee, the solution seems as clear as the nose on your face. This is because your brain is not firing on all cylinders in the wee hours of the morning. Conversely, when 4:00 PM rolls around, you are dragging, barely able to put one foot in front of the other or string two logical sentences together. Clearly, this is not the best time of day to be making important decisions or engaging in serious conversations.

- The majority of us experience our peak emotional and physical operating effectiveness in the late morning/early afternoon and early evening. This is the time of day when we are at our most creative and our most energetic. Our critical thinking skills, decision making, problem solving and negotiating abilities are at their peak. This is the time of day when we should be doing the 'heavy mental lifting.'

If you do not know what your natural emotional and energy rhythms are, try tracking them for a week or so. Note the times of day when you feel your best, and become aware of the times when you feel like you are dragging. Most likely, you will see a rhythmic trend, day after day. This will help you establish your natural rhythm and guide you in setting up a schedule for your day.

Almost as important as knowing your daily rhythms, are knowing the daily rhythms of those around you. Perhaps the most important person is your spouse or partner. Is he/she a morning person, or a night owl? Once you know this, you will know the best time of day to tackle tough issues—and when to avoid them.

It is also helpful to know the daily rhythm of others in your life, including your children, your co-workers, and your boss. Knowing the best (and worst) time of day to approach your kids about completing their chores, to deal with co-workers about sensitive work issues, or to approach your boss about getting a raise, will certainly make your life easier. By the way, whether they are consciously aware of it or not, your kids are fully aware of your daily rhythm. They know the best and worst times to hit you up for money or ask to stay over at a friend's house!

Personally, I follow the typical daily rhythm cycle. When I get up in the morning, I need to have a cup of coffee, do my stretching, and have breakfast before I can even complete full sentences. After the second cup of coffee, around 10 AM I am ready for the day and I start doing the tasks that require my full creativity and attention—like working on my speeches, writing, managing household issues, working on projects, returning phone calls, etc. Around 2 PM, as my energy and brainpower start to fade, I execute routine tasks, such as clearing out email, researching material for my books and speeches, completing household chores, and working out. At around 4 PM, I usually read for a while and take a power nap. After I get up, and after some more caffeine, I experience another surge of energy and do some more work around the house. I take Orbit for a walk, or complete another project. By 10 PM I am done for the day and wind down by reading a novel, biography or a historical book.

On the other hand, Kristi is a night owl. At 9 PM she is just getting wound up. I am amazed at how much she accomplishes late at night. Fortunately, we are aware of each other's daily rhythms, and we respect them. Kristi knows that talking to me about anything significant late at night is like talking to a log, a very sleepy log.

Implementing any or all of the models discussed here can help you reduce negative thinking, thus setting a foundation for a more positive attitude that will help you to be more productive, creative, healthier and happier in every aspect of your life.

"I have for many years endeavored to make this vital truth clear; and still people marvel when I tell them that I am happy. They imagine that my limitations weigh heavily upon my spirit, and chain me to the rock of despair. Yet, it seems to me, happiness has very little to do with the senses. If we make up our minds that this is a drab and purposeless universe, it will be that, and nothing else. On the other hand, if we believe that the earth is ours, and that the sun and moon hang in the sky for our delight, there will be joy upon the hills and gladness in the fields because the Artist in our souls glorifies creation. Surely, it gives dignity to life to believe that we are born into this world for noble ends, and that we have a higher destiny than can be accomplished within the narrow limits of this physical life."

~ Helen Keller

Chapter 10
Resiliency with a Less Than Perfect Brain

Millions of Americans struggle with cognitive issues on a daily basis. Cognitive issues can stem from birth defects, injuries, illnesses, diseases, car accidents, alcohol, or drugs. Regardless of how the cognitive issues were acquired, these people must learn to live with their challenges and find a new 'normal'. Kristi and I have each suffered from brain injuries and we have been caregivers to a brain-injured person. Therefore, I feel we are uniquely qualified to comment on this condition. I believe that individuals fighting cognitive problems can overcome their challenges and sometimes become more resilient than those who have never dealt with these issues. Current research indicates that the human brain has much more recuperative abilities than once believed.

In his book, *The Brain that Changes Itself*, Dr. Norman Doidge, a psychiatrist, explains how doctors have discovered that the human brain has the ability to change itself to overcome mental illness and brain injuries. This is considered to be one of the biggest breakthroughs in understanding the human brain. Experts now believe that our thoughts can turn our genes on and off, altering our brain anatomy. This remarkable discovery is known as Neuroplasticity, which is the ability of the brain to change itself without the use of surgery or medication. The term is from *neuro,* meaning the neurons in our brain and nervous systems and *plasticity,* meaning changeable, malleable or modifiable.

It was once thought that the brain was a stationary organ that could not change. Mainstream medical doctors and scientists believed that brain anatomy was permanent. Most of these experts assumed that the only change the brain made after childhood, was a long period of decline.

They also believed that when brain cells were injured or died, they could not be healed and the brain was incapable of altering the way it currently processed information. Scientists believed that people who were born with brain limitations or who sustained brain damage would remain that way for life.

There were three major reasons that physicians believed that the brain could not change itself:

- They rarely witnessed brain-damaged patients making full recoveries.
- They were unable to see the living brain's microscopic activity.
- They theorized that the brain is simply an amazing machine without the ability to change and grow.

Doctors believed if a patient failed to progress, it was because the brain was hard-wired. Hard-wiring was a concept from the unchangeable brain theory.

In the 1970's, scientists discovered that when one part of the brain was damaged, another part of the brain could take over and accomplish the task. Damaged brain cells are sometimes able to repair and grow new brain cells via a process called neurogenesis. Oftentimes, when brain cells die, the brain can find new neuro-pathways to bypass the brain cells that have died. Scientists also discovered that children are not always stuck with the mental capacity with which they are born. According to Dr. Doidge, the neuro-plasticity revolution will affect our understanding of grief, relationships, love, sex, addictions, culture, technology, psychotherapy and how we learn.

His book cites many real life examples of how this revolution has already affected us. Here are some examples:

Side effects from an antibiotic damaged a woman's vestibular system, the part of the brain that allows balance. Due to this damage, she felt she was perpetually falling and had problems standing and walking. Doctors attached a thin plastic strip with electrodes to her tongue that simulated the feeling of having liquid in her mouth. This provided a signal to her brain that she could balance, which then allowed her to stand and walk.

With the use of PET scans, doctors were able to take 'before' pictures of the brains of those affected with Obsessive Compulsive Disorder (OCD). They tried several different modalities of psychotherapy and then took 'after' pictures. This technique allowed doctors to develop the most effective therapeutic modalities of 'talk therapy' to improve the overall brain function.

With the help of neuroplasticity, a woman who was born with the use of only half of her brain, was able to achieve massive brain re-organization. The healthy half of her brain was able to compensate for the damaged half.

ᘕ

Traumatic brain injuries, or TBIs, are quickly becoming one of the major contributors of cognitive problems in the United States. According to the Center for Disease Control (CDC), TBIs account for almost 30% of all injury related deaths. It is estimated that 138 people die every day from injuries that include TBIs. Brain injury survivors may face mild effects that last only a few days or severe problems that last a lifetime. A TBI is caused when the head hits an object or when an object pierces the skull and enters brain tissue. Effects of TBI can include impaired thinking or memory, movement, sensation (e.g., vision or hearing), or emotional functioning (e.g., abnormal personality changes, depression). These issues not only affect the person suffering from the brain injury, but the families and communities of those around the person.

How big is the problem? According to the CDC. In 2010, about 2.5 million emergency department visits, hospital-izations, or deaths were associated with TBIs—either alone or in combination with other injuries. TBIs contributed to the deaths of more than 50,000 people. TBI was a diagnosis in more than 280,000 hospitalizations and 2.2 million emergency department visits. These consisted of TBI alone or TBI in combination with other injuries.

Far and away, the greatest causes of TBIs in the U.S. are falls. While not very dramatic, they account for over 40% of all TBIs. Falls disproportionately affect the youngest and oldest age groups.

The second largest cause of TBI is unintentional blunt force trauma, or being hit in the head with an object. This accounts for 15% of TBIs.

The third largest cause of TBI is motor vehicle accidents, accounting for 14% of the total. These accidents are the number one cause of hospitalizations for adolescents and adults between the ages of 18 and 44.

Society is slowly beginning to understand the devastating effects brain injuries have on individuals, families and the country. Up to this point, it seems we, the general public, have simply swept the problem under the rug and ignored it. Ignoring the problem is easy as long as you have been unaffected by a personal brain injury or haven't had a loved one who has suffered from one.

In the recent past, scientists' lack of knowledge about how the brain worked, prevented them from understanding how to effectively treat brain injuries. Today, the media is replete with stories of individuals who have suffered brain injuries. This has done wonders in educating the public on this devastating issue.

ᘒ

Brain injuries are one of the invisible wounds of war and have become the signature injury of the conflicts in Iraq and Afghanistan. Medical improvements in combat zones are saving the lives of many soldiers who previously would have died. The flip side of that coin is that many are returning home with lifelong disabilities. Based on existing data, veterans' advocates believe that between 10 and 20% of veterans have some level of brain injury. This means that of the 2.7 million veterans of these wars, 270,000 to 540,000 are suffering from a brain injury.

Soldiers returning from World War II with brain injuries were said to be 'shell shocked'. We now understand this to be varying degrees of brain injuries and post-traumatic stress disorders (PTSD). These soldiers came home to their families and were presented with virtually no information on how to treat the problem. A better understanding of the complexities of brain injuries is permitting today's veterans to more effectively deal with this disability.

᠙

A dark cloud hung over the 2015 National Football League (NFL) hall of fame induction ceremony in Canton, Ohio as Junior Seau's daughter, Sydney, posthumously accepted his induction. Seau committed suicide on May 2, 2012 at the age of 43 after playing fifteen years in the NFL. Seau suffered from chronic traumatic encephalopathy (CTE), a degenerative brain disease common to athletes who have absorbed frequent blows to the head. Symptoms of CTE include memory loss, depression and dementia. Researchers at Boston University, who pioneered the study of CTE., examined 91 brains of former NFL players and found chronic traumatic encephalopathy in 87 of them. Unfortunately, the examinations can only be done posthumously.

The NFL is finally starting to acknowledge some of the brain injuries that players' suffer from. In a 2013 suit against the NFL, 4,500 former players, including Tony Dorsett, Jim McMahon and Eric Dickerson, sued the league accusing the organization of covering up the long-term health risks caused by head injuries. The league agreed to pay a settlement of $1 billion. Experts believe that the NFL will be forced to change the rules of the game to reduce these injuries.

᠙

On Jan. 29, 2006, 27 days after Bob Woodruff took the position as the co-anchor of ABC World News Tonight, he was nearly killed when a roadside bomb struck his vehicle while on assignment near Taji, Iraq.

Embedded with the military, his convoy was damaged by an improvised explosive device (IED). Woodruff was wearing body armor and was in a tank, but his head, neck, and shoulders were exposed during the blast.

The blast knocked Woodruff unconscious as rocks and metal pierced his face, jaw, and neck. As a result of the explosion, Woodruff suffered a severe brain injury.

After waking up from a thirty-six-day, medically-induced coma, Woodruff could not remember the names of his children, or that he had twins. He also suffered from aphasia, the inability to find words. After an intense program of cognitive rehabilitation, he was able to regain many of the skills he had lost.

Woodruff returned to the air 13 months after his injury, telling his story in a documentary called *To Iraq and Back: Bob Woodruff Reports*. He has also shared his story in his book, *In an Instant: A Family's Journey of Love and Healing.*

გ

Actor/comedian Tracy Morgan, an alumni of 'Saturday Night Live' and star of '30 Rock', suffered a traumatic brain injury, broken leg and broken ribs when the limo he was riding in was hit on the New Jersey Turnpike by a truck on June 7, 2014. When interviewed by Matt Lauer on the Today Show, Morgan said that he has his good days, and then he has bad days and forgets things. "There are times where I get the headaches, and the nose bleeds. I won't even let my lady know because I don't want her to be worried about it," Morgan said. After more than a year of intense therapy and rehabilitation, Morgan is getting his life back on track. He was recently married. (He wanted to be able to walk down the aisle without the use of a cane.) He also hosted an episode of Saturday Night Live in 2015.

გ

A quick word to you motorcycle riders who choose not to wear a helmet. I previously rode motorcycles. I know what a hassle helmets are. They are hot and they make your head sweaty. But, it is only temporary. You can fix your hair later. A brain injury is for life.

Brain injuries are categorized as either mild, moderate or severe. Even though mild sounds harmless, it is a serious injury and requires immediate attention and accurate diagnosis. In the weeks, months and yes, even years after the accident, I suffered many of the typical symptoms associated with a severe brain injury. In those early days, I was often confused and disoriented. I did not remember the accident, the names we had chosen for our babies, or even the fact that we were expecting twins. The neuropsychologist I worked with would tell me a story and have me repeat it. I was quite certain that I was regurgitating it just as it was told to me. But Kristi, listening in the next room, was heartbroken that I couldn't put anything in sequential order. The other odd thing that was apparent to those around me was that often, as I was having a conversation with someone, a word would pop into the sentence that wasn't related to what I was talking about. Sometimes I would notice it and sometimes I was completely unaware of it. Headaches were a common occurrence. I never knew how debilitating a migraine was until I suffered from one. I also 'saw' things that weren't there. For example, every time I looked at Kristi, I saw a halo above her head. Then later it became a towel wrapped around her hair. I believe part of the reason I bounced back from the accident is that I was so 'hard-headed' that I was determined to prove everybody wrong. One strange development was my long-term memory improved! I started remembering my old phone numbers and addresses. Sleep problems were one of the most difficult issues I had to face after my brain injury. Being unable to get a restful night of sleep affected my entire day. My daily rhythms were so out of whack, that it is a miracle I was able to function at all. Because I was sleep deprived, I had problems concentrating, following conversations and processing information. I started taking an antidepressant. Taking an antidepressant and literally forcing myself to stay awake during the day eventually allowed me to regulate my sleep patterns. Finally, I was able to replace the antidepressant with St. John's Wort, then melatonin. Along with the techniques I outlined in Chapter 8, I was able to get a good night's sleep every night. Getting an optimal amount of sleep made every day easier. My mental processing skills improved. I was more productive; my memory was enhanced; I was more creative and, I'm sure I was a whole lot easier to live with.

ଛ

It was once thought that any healing of the brain would occur within the first year. Experts now believe that the brain can continue to improve for five years, and sometimes beyond. That first year, however, is by far the most critical. Kristi and I were quite the pair in those early days. It took both of us to keep the bus going in the right direction. Rocky's line to Adrian from the first 'Rocky' movie fit us. The line is, "We filled gaps."

Most people didn't recognize Kristi's brain injury. Since she suffered no other major disabilities, except lingering effects of her crushed foot, most of the attention was given to me and my blindness. But, make no mistake; she suffered real issues. Her short term, and long-term, memory was almost nonexistent. It was like every day was a brand new day, with little memory of the previous day. She had problems processing simple menial tasks and she had a very limited attention span.

For example, when we would go through a drive through to get something to eat, she could not remember her food order, much less the order for the boys and me. I would have to tell her each item so she could repeat it to the person taking the order. She also bought items, put them in drawers and forgot they were there.

Three years after the accident, Kristi began graduate school. That first paper she was required to write, which should have taken a few hours, took days and days. Every evening she would do some writing, then go to sleep. The next morning, when she picked up what she had written, she could not remember having written it the day before.

I once heard a neurological researcher say that if you see one brain injury, you have seen one brain injury. Brain injuries are all uniquely different, and are impossible to put into a nice little box. Even a rather mild blow to the head can cause serious cognitive problems and prevent the victim from returning to a normal life. Conversely, head injuries that appear severe enough to be fatal can leave the individual with only what appears to be minor symptoms. I experienced a real life reminder of this baffling phenomenon.

I was giving a presentation to a support group for the brain-injured. After the presentation, a young lady came up to speak to Kristi and me. It was immediately apparent that she had severe cognitive issues: problems speaking, difficulty completing thoughts, and struggling to find the correct words. As she was speaking, I surmised that she had suffered some kind of horrific accident. But that was not the case at all. She had been running outside to greet her boyfriend and miscalculated how far a 2x4 piece of lumber was sticking out of the back of a truck. She hit it head on. On our way home from the presentation, Kristi and I were both stunned at the level of her brain injury as compared to ours. We were hit head-on by a car traveling at fifty miles an hour, but she had only run into a board. How could this be explained? How was it possible that we were able to regain so much of our cognitive abilities when she was not? It is just an example of one of the many mysteries of the brain.

ଝ

Whether you have suffered a brain injury or just want to sharpen your mental skills, here are some basic tips to get your brain firing on all cylinders.

Put your brain on an exercise program

Start doing crossword puzzles, brainteasers and mental games. This will help create new neuro-pathways in the brain, which will keep it sharp. Visit sites like lumosity.com, as mentioned in Chapter 8. Another idea is to perform daily activities with your non-dominant hand, such as brushing your teeth and combing your hair, or journaling. Do anything to keep your brain sharp.

Take up new interests

Learn some new activities, such as how to play a musical instrument or speak a new language. In addition to improving your brain power, this will also make it easier for you to learn new concepts in the future.

Choose healthy brain foods

Be sure to incorporate lots of brain healthy foods into your diet such as omega 3 fatty acids, blueberries, nuts, avocados and fish. Eating healthy foods improves cognitive functioning. For a detailed list of brain healthy foods, see this article: webmd.com/diet/eat-smart-healthier-brain

Do something innovative

Incorporate new activities into your daily routine. Take up a new exercise program, such as yoga or spinning. The additional mental stimulation will invigorate your brain. As an added bonus, these activities are as good for your body as they are for your brain.

Socialize

We are naturally social creatures, and designed to interact with each other on a regular basis. Socializing helps us to stay on top of our game. Recent studies show that older adults who are socially active have sharper cognitive skills than those who are less socially active.

Volunteer your time and talent

Volunteering to help others improves your mental attitude and your physical health. Rolling up your sleeves to benefit others does wonders for your outlook on life. It also makes your community a better place to live.

 භ

Kristi and I do not for one minute take for granted how fortunate we are to have accomplished what we have since our brain injuries. If you or a loved one is dealing with cognitive problems of any kind, I strongly encourage you to seek the help of a neurologist and to consider counseling by a licensed therapist. A therapist can give you tools to accept who you are and help you to be the best that you can be. There is a rewarding life after cognitive problems. I know. We are living it.

Chapter 11
Leap List

Completing one's 'Bucket List' is a popular concept in today's world. Movies have been produced, books have been written and there are countless entries on Facebook and personal blogs about how to accomplish one. A 'Bucket List' is quite simply a list of personal goals one wants to complete before he/she dies. I am not a big fan of the 'Bucket List.' To me, it is a rather depressing concept. My 'Bucket List' includes finding a nursing home with friendly nurses, a comfortable bed and decent food.

My first problem with the 'Bucket List' is that none of us know when we are going to die, which makes it difficult to assign a time table for completing the goals. It could be tomorrow; it could be fifty years. Second, it puts our 'to do' date all the way out to the end of our lives, thus making it easier to keep putting off attaining the goals. It turns from a 'things we want to do before we kick the bucket' to a 'kick the can down the road' list.

I much prefer the **Leap List** model. To complete a Leap List, you designate a specific time in the future to accomplish each goal. This pre-designated date can be before a major milestone in your life, such as your wedding, purchasing a home, the birth of your first child, before or after becoming an empty nester, and before or after retirement.

The goal date can also be a pre-designated timeframe, such as one, three or five years. Anything over ten years should probably be re-evaluated. Is it really that important to you? If so, you should consider shortening the timeframe.

Once the goal and timeframe are established, put a concrete plan in place to make sure you have a workable blueprint to successfully accomplish it. Be sure to use the goal setting model that works best for you, such as the SMART model discussed in Chapter 5.

If you are really serious about accomplishing a Leap List goal, assign an accountability partner to check in with you periodically to see how you are progressing. You should have several 'Leap Lists' dealing with the many facets of your life, including career, family, spiritual, recreational, travel, hobbies, volunteerism, and health. Keep in mind that this is a flexible list and may require some fine tuning as time goes on.

I think most people have every intention of completing a Leap List, but never get around to actually writing one. At my presentations, I give the audience a few minutes to come up with one Leap List goal. Then I have several people share the goal with the group. This is one of my favorite parts of the presentation. I never know what goals the audience will come up with. Sometimes they are educational (finish a college degree, learn a second language), recreational (run a marathon, start working out) or career (put together a resume and get a job in which I am passionate). Whatever the goal is, I believe sharing a goal with the group motivates the individual to accomplish the goal.

I like to think that this segment of my presentation has encouraged people to get busy and attain a personal dream. For that reason, I would like to encourage you to take a few minutes to get started on your own Leap List. Set aside some time for your own hopes and dreams and look at this as you would look at a homework assignment.

While contemplating the list, be creative. Think about all of the possibilities without being too logical. That side of the equation will take care of itself soon enough. Be sure to keep the Resiliency Triangle in mind while developing the list.

Develop a positive attitude.

- Be committed to your goals.
- Enlist a strong support group.

While some people know what is on their Leap List, others have not given it a thought. Many people spend a lot of time pushing through their work week, day-by-day, but spend little to no time focusing on their hopes and dreams. Do not put it off any longer.

Put together your Leap List

And, may I suggest, make it a group project. Do it with your family, work colleagues, friends or church group. It is a fun, possibly life-changing mission. Working on your list with others provides you with an accountability partner who will help you make your dream a reality.

Suggested Leap List outline

- Category (career, personal, hobby, etc.):
- Leap List item (finish college, learn Spanish, play guitar, etc.):
- Analysis (Is the Leap List goal realistic? Can you afford it? Do you have the time you need to commit to the project to make it happen?)

If so, develop a flow chart to help you execute it. Include dates and timelines, projected cost, etc. Be sure to include others that can assist you in accomplishing the goal (spouse, family members, friends, co-workers, etc.)

Example

Let's say one of your Leap List goals is to ski the Swiss Alps. Run it through the Leap List model above.

- Is it practical?
- Do you have someone who would go with you? Your spouse? Friend? A group?
- What would the cost be? Get online and check airline fares and hotel/chalet cost. Check lift ticket and food and beverage costs. How much will you need to put away every week to afford the trip?
- How long do you want the trip to be? A week? A month?
- Can you get the time off work? What time of year do you want to go?

If everything checks out, put a date on the calendar and start working on your plan. Before you know it, you will be swooshing down the slopes of the Swiss Alps!

ɮ

Many people do not know what goals they should put on their 'Leap List.' Perhaps they are just too busy to sit down and think about it, or they aren't very creative, or they have listened to naysayers tell them that it cannot be done. The internet provides unlimited possibilities. One suggestion I have is a website called curious.com. On this site, you can choose from hundreds of activities, skills or hobbies. Some of the lessons or instructional videos are free, others have a minimal fee. To whet your appetite for a Leap List item, here are a few examples that I found interesting:

- **Career-** Land your dream job or start your own business.
- **Communication-** Learn a foreign language.
- **Hobby-** Pick up jewelry making or woodworking.
- **Food-** Teach yourself to cook healthy meals.
- **Health-** Discover new exercise programs, like spinning.
- **Sports-** Train yourself to run obstacle courses.
- **Life-** Take up square dancing.
- **Music-** Learn to play the piano or harmonica.
- **Photography-** Become an expert at digital photography.
- **Tech-** Teach yourself how to record and mix music.

ɮ

Take the first step to *start your own Leap List.* You have a new, exciting, fulfilling life out there waiting for you. After all, you only live once. *(Hey, wait a minute. That is the title of the next chapter!)*

Chapter 12
You Only Live Once

"I find the great thing in this world is not so much where we stand,
as in what direction we are moving—we must sail sometimes with the
wind and sometimes against it-but we must sail, and not drift,
nor lie at anchor."

~ Oliver Wendell Holmes, Jr.

It is no secret that time flies. As you age, it seems to fly even faster. I recently heard an explanation that seems to be logical. When you were ten years old, one year made up 10% of the time you had spent on this earth. You had no real memory of the first three years (30% of your life). It seemed to take forever for Christmas to roll around. The month of December seemed to last a year by itself. By the time you are (or were) 50 years old, one year makes up only 2% of your life. Everything on the annual calendar has happened to you fifty times already. The anticipation and the newness have worn off, and your brain experiences more routines, which gives the feeling that time is passing faster and faster. You are thinking, "It's Christmas already? Didn't we just have Christmas six months ago?

How did it get so late so soon?
It's night before its afternoon.
December is here before its June.
My goodness how the time has flewn.
How did it get so late so soon?"

~ Dr. Seuss

You are certainly feeling this time acceleration in every phase of your life. It seems like the years are flying by so fast, your life goals can't keep up. So many of those hopes and dreams that you once had, are now so far back on the back burner, they are getting cobwebs.

An exercise that may help you re-prioritize your life is a **YOLO** review. (For those of you born before 1980, **YOLO** stands for "You Only Live Once").

The concept is this; Take a look back in your life. Did you accomplish your hopes and dreams, or are these dreams still on your to do list? If an item has been on your 'to do list' for ten years, maybe it's time to change the goal, take it off the list or finally do it. But, make a choice and stop feeling remorseful that you haven't yet done it.

The YOLO check list

Think back 10 years—unless you are over 50, then think back 20 years.

- What was your status (married, single or complicated)?
- Where were you working?
- Where did you live? Rent or own?
- What were your hobbies? Interests?
- What was your physical condition?
- What was your financial status?
- What level of education had you achieved?
- Where were you spiritually?

Now go back through the above list and think about your goals for each item at that time. If you have managed to accomplish those goals, congratulations! Pat yourself on the back. You deserve it.

If some of your goals have not been achieved, examine each goal and figure out why you were unsuccessful. Was the goal unrealistic? Did you simply fail to put together an effective plan? Should you have assigned an accountability partner?

By looking back at your past goals, both those achieved and those you have not, you can get a good idea of how you can effectively set goals for the future. Look for trends. Why did you accomplish some goals but not others? Were you more efficacious with your personal goals, but not your career goals? As you set goals for the future, be certain that you examine what worked in the past and utilize those tools.

So why is it important to look back while setting goals, or for that matter to even set goals at all? And, what do I know about setting goals? To be quite honest, I was never very good at setting goals before my accident. But, what I have since learned, is that life is very fragile. You only have one go around on this earth. So, it is up to you, and no one else, what you do with your life. Don't take for granted your ability to be in control of your own destiny. In a split second, a monkey wrench could be thrown into your plans. Monkey wrenches can take on many different faces. They can be self-induced. They can be perpetrated by others wishing you ill will. Or they can be totally out of your control. You only live once. It's up to you to make it count.

☙

A common desire is that you will get to the end of your life and you will have done all of the things that you wanted to do and accomplished all of the goals that you have set for yourself.

Fulfilling your hopes and dreams is not a project that you can commence on your deathbed. You do not want to get to the end of your days and wish you had done things differently. Resilient people are quite adept at checking off items from their 'to do' list as they complete each one.

It is not surprising that most people have similar regrets toward the end of their lives. Proof of this comes from Bronnie Ware, an Australian nurse, who for years provided hospice care to terminal patients who had decided to die at home. She noted that people facing mortality became more realistic and honest about their own lives. While discussing regrets, she noticed that those who were dying came up with common themes. In her book, *Top Five Regrets of the Dying*, she shares this list.

1. I wish I'd had the courage to live a life true to myself not what others expected of me.
   So many times people live their life based on other's expectations. They often end up unhappy and

disillusioned. Choosing what you love can make your life rich and rewarding.

2. I wish I hadn't worked so hard.

   It seems to be the American way to work hard and make a lot of money. People from some foreign countries embrace the concept of working hard and playing hard. In Europe, many people take the entire month of August off. In Mexico shops are closed during 'siesta time'. Hawaiian Islands they call this 'island time'. Everything is slowed way down.

3. I wish I could have expressed my feelings.

   Many people avoid conflict rather than saying what they feel. They believe bottling their emotions somehow makes them a 'bigger person'. What they fail to comprehend is that hiding their emotions causes sickness, and it also keeps people 'arm's length'.

4. I wish I had stayed in touch with my friends.

   Often, as people are facing death, they realize that their old friends have fallen to the wayside. They regret not keeping those friends around so that they could reminisce about the past and share their fears

5. I wish that I had allowed myself to be happier.

   Many people truly believe that life 'comes at them'. They believe that some people are just luckier than others. Many do not realize until the end of their life that happiness is a choice.

&

To avoid finding yourself in the position of facing death with serious regrets, put a plan in place to prevent it. As discussed earlier, you only live once. So here are some useful tips to help you whittle down your regret list:

Live the life YOU want to live

"There is no passion to be found in settling for a life that is less than the one you are capable of living."

~Nelson Mandela

Many people end up following a career or life path that their parents, spouse or another influential person in their life wished for them to live, only to discover that they are not happy.

These people may be indifferent about their life, or they may absolutely hate it, but they are certainly not passionate about it. Over the years, I have met many people who have chosen law, or medicine, insurance or engineering because their parents pushed them into that field. And they absolutely detest their profession. I often ask these people; why don't you get out of it? The answer is usually pretty simple. They either believe they are making too much money to change professions, or believe that they must stay in order to support the family business. But, the bottom line is that they continue to do what they do because of *FEAR*.

On the other hand, I have met people who are absolutely passionate about what they do. You can hear it in their voices and see it on their faces. Their positive attitudes about how they are living their lives is absolutely contagious.

What is it that puts you in one category or the other? Luck? Fate? Circumstances? The answer may be complicated. The truth is that wherever you end up is your CHOICE. If you are dissatisfied with your current status in life, you can change it. By employing some of the techniques in this book, you can look at your options and seek a career or a lifestyle that you are passionate about. Take a career aptitude test (you are never too old!); see what jumps out at you. If you have always longed to live by the ocean, start looking at real estate listings and job postings in beach cities. Then, prioritize that list. Finally, put together your plan to make it happen. It may take you 5 years. It may take you 10, but living the life you want to live, a life you won't regret, is certainly worth the investment.

"Twenty years from now you will be more disappointed by the things you didn't do than by the things you did."

~ Mark Twain

Learn from your mistakes

Have you ever started down one road, only to discover it was not a viable option, and then decided to never stick out your neck again? The list is long and storied of the successful people who have failed, then failed again. But, with tenacity and determination, these people eventually achieved their goals. You can do the same thing. Do not waste time regretting what may have been. Just roll up your sleeves, redesign the plan, and try again.

> "The greatest glory in living lies not in never falling,
> but in rising every time we fall."
>
> ~Nelson Mandela

Do not work so hard

A pastor at my church once said that he had often sat at peoples' bedsides as they were near the end of their lives. He stated that he had never heard, "I wish I had spent more time at work." Rather, they all mourned the time that they had lost for the things that truly mattered: family, friends, hobbies and generally making the world a better place.

I have friends and acquaintances (mostly attorneys and doctors, now that I think about it) who routinely put in 80, 90, even 100-hour work weeks. When people put in those kinds of hours, every other part of their life is negatively affected...their bodies, their minds and their relationships.

Recently, I read an article that stated law firms are having a difficult time hiring new college graduates as associates. In the past, it was understood that a new attorney was expected to work 100 hours a week before they could earn junior partner status. But, many of today's law school graduates are choosing quality of life over a high-powered career path. They are upfront and tell prospective employers that they are only willing to work 40 hour weeks. They are not as concerned about making junior partner as they are with enjoying their life. Bravo!

145

There is also a groundswell of consideration in reducing the incredible hours that new medical school graduates are forced to put in during their residency programs. Stories of sleep deprived interns making costly medical mistakes are often the result of this antiquated system. Experts are coming to the conclusion that this training method serves no useful purpose...especially for patients.

Spend more time with your kids

There is an old saying that children are only young once. Unfortunately, many of us do not fully comprehend that concept until our children are packing their belongings for college. Set aside time in your day to spend quality, and quantity time with your kids. I know your day is filled with important business meetings, social commitments and golf outings. But as the years go by, you will eventually forget about all of the things that you thought were important. What you will remember however, is the special time that you spent with your kids. Those times do not have to be expensive vacations. They can be as basic as swimming in the backyard pool or playing ball at the neighborhood park. The important thing is that kids have a mom or a dad who gives them undivided attention. So, put down your computer and cell phone for a few minutes and be in the moment with your kids.

Share your feelings

Many people live their lives in fear; fear of being vulnerable, fear of getting hurt, fear of being wrong. But, when we share our feelings with another person, we meet them heart to heart and develop a deeper connection with them that is a much more fulfilling relationship than a superficial one.

Keep in touch with friends

Many of you have most likely, at one time or another, have said to a friend, "We need to get together; let's grab lunch or a cup of coffee." Next thing you know, five years, ten years or even twenty, have sailed by and you still have not made time for lunch with that old friend. Before you know it, you have totally lost contact.

Make a dedicated effort to make those moments a reality. Instead of just saying, "We need to...," set up a specific time and date. This will increase the odds of the date taking place. If you do not have the time, or the inclination to physically see an old friend, make an effort to reach that person by phone or online. Shoot them an email from out of the blue. Send them a note on Facebook. They will love to hear from you.

A friend of mine used to call me once a month. He had attended a seminar where the speaker suggested making a list of the people you want to keep in touch with and put it on your calendar. Once a month, he would call me for no reason at all and say, "You came up on my day timer." We would talk for only a few minutes, but I felt more connected to him because I knew what he was doing. When he first started calling, I thought it was kind of a waste of time. Busy running my insurance agency, I felt I did not have the time to spare. I later came to value those few minutes once a month. Then, my friend passed away. There would be no more calls. I really appreciate those times when he connected with me. The lesson: reach out to your friends—while you still can.

> "Friendship is unnecessary, like philosophy, like art. It has no survival value; rather it is one of those things that give value to survival."
> ~ C.S. Lewis

Happiness is a choice; choose well

We all choose what kind of attitude we wish to present to the world. Will we be positive or negative? In Chapter 4, we discussed the concept of resilient people having positive attitudes, and we covered some of the keys to unlocking and utilizing a positive attitude.

Our accident gave Kristi and me a unique perspective on who we were and who we wanted to be. We were only 33 and 37 years old when we had our accident. We both believe that

God allowed us to live in order to find our purpose. Then we set about doing it.

Do not wait for a near fatal event in your life for a wakeup call. Start living the life of your dreams today!

There is no power on earth that can neutralize
the influence of a high, pure, simple and useful life.
~ Booker T. Washington

Eulogy

I know, I know... the last chapter of a book is supposed to be called the epilogue. I have chosen to title our last chapter the *eulogy*. I have done so because I want you to 'play the movie forward'. What do you want to have completed when you leave this earthly life?

You only have so many days to undertake all of the things that you wish to accomplish. Look at it this way; during your lifetime, you will have a limited number of days to wake up in the morning and eat a bowl of cereal. Let's call it 'Life Cereal'. Assume that your adult life begins when you are 18 years old and you live until you are 78 years old. That equals 60 years, times that by 365 days in a year, and you get a total of 21,900 days. This means that if you get up every morning and eat a bowl of Life Cereal, you will have consumed 21,900 bowls of cereal in your Life. The mark you leave on the world will be determined by how you choose to spend your day.

So, how many bowls of Life Cereal have you already eaten? How many of your lifetime goals have you already achieved? If you are young and just getting started on your Life Cereal then, good for you! You have plenty of time to work on your life résumé. But, do not procrastinate. You will be shocked at how fast those bowls of cereal disappear—just ask someone who is down to the bottom of their box.

If you are well into your total allotment of Life Cereal, you can hopefully look back over your time on this earth and see many of your hopes and dreams that came to fruition or observe that you are well on your way to accomplishing them. If you are coming up short, look at what 'tools' previously worked for you. Then apply them today so you can finish strong.

What if you just have a few bowls of Life Cereal left and there are some items left on your 'Leap List'? Should you just throw in the towel and assume that they will never get done?

Absolutely not! I have read many stories of people who accomplished great things late in their life. Some people do their best work while eating their last few hundred bowls of Life Cereal. Why not be one of them?

What will your eulogy be? What do you hope people will say about you? Will it include all of the many wonderful, lifetime achievements that you attained? Or, will life get in the way of you fulfilling all of your dreams? That, my friend is up to you!

The Dash
A poem by Linda Ellis

I read of a man who stood to speak
At the funeral of a friend.
He referred to the dates on her tombstone
From the beginning to the end.
He noted that first came her date of her birth
And spoke the following date with tears,
But he said what mattered most of all
Was the dash between those years.
For that dash represents all the time
That she spent alive on earth.
And now only those who loved her
Know what that little line is worth.
For it matters not how much we own;
The cars, the house, the cash,
What matters is how we live and love
And how we spend our dash.
So think about this long and hard.
Are there things you'd like to change?
For you never know how much time is left,
That can still be rearranged.
If we could just slow down enough
To consider what's true and real,
And always try to understand
The way other people feel,
And be less quick to anger,
And show appreciation more,
And love the people in our lives
Like we've never loved before.
If we treat each other with respect,
And more often wear a smile,
Remembering that this special dash
Might only last a little while.
So, when your eulogy is being read,
With your life's actions to rehash,
Would you be proud of the things they say?
About how you spent your dash?

About the Authors

Steve Welker is the author of *The World at my Fingertips* and is a motivational speaker. He graduated from Arizona State University with a bachelor's degree in business and a field of specialization in insurance. He currently serves on the Board of Directors for the Arizona Center for the Blind and Visually Impaired, is an advocate for The Guide Dogs of the Desert and a member of the Chandler Lions Club.

Dr. Kristina Welker earned her Bachelor's degree in Communications, her Master's degree in Counseling, and her Doctorate in Psychology. She is a licensed professional counselor in private practice and has written practical advice articles for the Ahwatukee Foothills News for over 14 years.

The Welkers currently reside in Chandler, Arizona.

Copies of this book are available on Steve's web site:
radicalresiliency.com

and on Dr. Kristina's website:
drkristinawelker.com

The World at My Fingertips

Steve Welker's first book is still available from the Welker websites (see prior page) and at Amazon.com. Here is a quick preview from someone you probably know.

"I always consider it a blessing when someone allows their story to find its way to the public through me. But Steve and Kristi Welker did more than bless us with their story. They softened our hearts and healed souls. They educated and empowered. They offered a quiet example of selflessness and hard-fought-for love that has sustained them."

Leeza Gibbons
From the Foreword

Notes:

Notes:

Notes:

Notes:

Notes:

Notes:

Notes:

Made in the USA
Middletown, DE
05 September 2018